SCROOBY MANOR-HOUSE.

The Story of the Pilgrims

By
Morton Dexter

HERITAGE BOOKS
2022

HERITAGE BOOKS
AN IMPRINT OF HERITAGE BOOKS, INC.

Books, CDs, and more—Worldwide

For our listing of thousands of titles see our website
at
www.HeritageBooks.com

A Facsimile Reprint
Published 2022 by
HERITAGE BOOKS, INC.
Publishing Division
5810 Ruatan Street
Berwyn Heights, Md. 20740

Copyright © 1894 Morton Dexter

Originally published:
Boston and Chicago
Congregational Sunday-School and Publishing Society

— Publisher's Notice —
In reprints such as this, it is often not possible to remove blemishes from the original. We feel the contents of this book warrant its reissue despite these blemishes and hope you will agree and read it with pleasure.

International Standard Book Number
Paperbound: 978-1-55613-356-5

TO

𝔗𝔥𝔢 𝔐𝔢𝔪𝔬𝔯𝔶 of

HENRY MARTYN DEXTER

PREFACE.

DURING the latter part of the year 1892 a number of companies, composed largely of young people, were formed in connection with Congregational churches in different parts of the United States for the study of the principles of Congregationalism and the history of the early Congregationalists. They took the name of Scrooby Clubs. The chapters of this book were written principally in order to aid such students and were printed week by week in The Congregationalist during the first six months of 1893 under the title Scrooby Club Sketches. They have been revised carefully and considerably expanded for republication as a book, and the twenty-fourth chapter is now added to the original series. They contain some facts believed to have been insufficiently, if at all, made known hitherto, although most of their material is familiar, particularly to special students of the subject. I dare not hope to have avoided errors entirely, but I have made conscientious endeavor to be accurate. This book has been written from the point of view of a loyal Congregationalist, but with a sincere wish to avoid unfairness or discourtesy towards others. Dates have been stated according to the New Style. For permission to use the pictures of Plymouth in 1622 and the Old Fort, I am indebted to the courtesy of A. S. Burbank, Esq., of Plymouth, Mass., dealer in books and in photographs specially connected with Pilgrim history, who owns their copyrights.

MORTON DEXTER.

BOSTON, May 26, 1894.

CONTENTS.

Chapter I.
The England which the Pilgrims Left 11

Chapter II.
Puritanism and Congregationalism 24

Chapter III.
Robert Browne 36

Chapter IV.
Congregational Publications and Martyrs 50

Chapter V.
Scrooby and Austerfield 61

Chapter VI.
William Brewster and William Bradford 72

Chapter VII.
John Robinson 83

Chapter VIII.
Other Scrooby Pilgrims and the Decision to Emigrate 97

Chapter IX.
The Emigration to Holland 107

Contents

Chapter X.
In Amsterdam 118

Chapter XI.
In Leyden 130

Chapter XII.
The Development of Congregationalism 142

Chapter XIII.
The Departure from Holland 151

Chapter XIV.
The Voyage to America 163

Chapter XV.
Other Pilgrim Leaders and their Compact 175

Chapter XVI.
First Explorations 189

Chapter XVII.
The Beginning of the Colony 200

Chapter XVIII.
The Further History of the First Year 212

Chapter XIX.
More Haps and Mishaps 222

Chapter XX.
Trembling in the Balance 234

Chapter XXI.
The Dawn of Better Days 245

Chapter XXII.
The Commercial History of the Colony 257

Chapter XXIII.
Succeeding Years 270

Chapter XXIV.
Early Life in the Colony 282

Chapter XXV.
Distinctions between the Plymouth and Bay Colonies 301

Chapter XXVI.
Subsequent Development of Congregationalism . . 315

Chapter XXVII.
Conclusion 326

THE STORY OF THE PILGRIMS.

CHAPTER I.

THE ENGLAND WHICH THE PILGRIMS LEFT.

THE purpose of this book is to state briefly and clearly the principal facts in the history of the Pilgrims. They were men and women of so much force of character and such noble and holy aims, they underwent such terrible trials in so heroic a manner, and they accomplished a work of such vital and enduring importance to mankind that the details of their history deserve to be known far more widely than at present. Much has been written about them, but there have been few attempts to tell their whole story in a simple and popularly intelligible manner, and comparatively recent researches have thrown additional light upon some facts in regard to them.

It is desirable to explain at the outset how there came to be any Pilgrims. People do not exile themselves from home and native land and expose themselves voluntarily to oppression, poverty, and the risk of death without the strongest reasons. The statement often made that the Pilgrims fled from England to Holland, and finally came to America in order to obtain freedom to worship God is true, but it affords no sufficient explanation of the manner and extent of the prohibition of this freedom at home in their time. A short study of the religious condition of England during the centuries immediately preceding their departure therefore is first in order.

At the middle of the fourteenth century the Roman Catholic Church, which possessed supreme spiritual control in England, had become shamefully corrupt and had lost public confidence in a very large degree, although still firmly retaining its power. The people were in a mood to listen to any one who should set forth a purer religion, and John Wycliff, the famous preacher, reformer, and translator of the Bible into English, brought about a great popular change towards what afterwards became known as Protestantism. His followers were called Lollards, and during the remainder of the century and the reign of King Henry V (1413–22) they grew rapidly in both number and influence.[1] But the power of the Roman Catholic Church still was too great to be overthrown completely. A reaction in its favor took place and the Lollards were so far suppressed that their beliefs could not be held safely except in secret.

The decisive break between England and the Papacy occurred in the time of King Henry VIII (1509–47). At about the year 1529 he desired a divorce from Queen Catherine. The Pope refused to grant it. England still was distinctly Roman Catholic, but Henry was determined and fearless, and at last he openly assumed headship over the English Church and formally severed its connection with the Papacy. This was the origin of the present Anglican Church, or Church of England.[2] But it did not render that church Protestant, and in later reigns it was temporarily reunited, at least nominally, with the Church of Rome. Yet Protestantism was able to take some advantage of the secession and began to revive, and most of the Protestants became known thenceforth as Puritans, because of their wish to purify and reform the State Church.

From this time on for a hundred years the history of religion in England is a record of almost constant oppression on the part of the Roman Catholic authorities and of bitter sufferings on the part of those who sympathized with Protestantism. Chancellor More, Bishop Fisher, and many others prosecuted all such persons actively. We can understand that penalties for neglect of the church fast days and for absence from confession and the sacrament may have been natural in those times, although we know that they often were excessive. But what is to be thought of punishing people for reading religious books, especially Tyndale's translation of the Bible, for teaching children the Lord's Prayer in English, and for condemning the notorious vices of many of the state clergymen! It was for precisely these and similar offenses that the English Roman Catholics persecuted their Puritan fellow citizens, and they carried their cruelties so far that they even burned not a few of their victims at the stake.[3]

Edward VI (1547-53) — "good King Edward" — was of a nobler spirit. He sympathized more with his Protestant subjects and the work of reform which they desired seemed well begun. But his reign was so short that little was accomplished, and his successor, "Bloody Mary" (1553-58) again recognized the Pope as the head of the Church on earth and was in full sympathy with the most bigoted and cruel Roman Catholics. The worst practices of Popery were revived and encouraged.[4] All married clergymen were ordered to put away their wives or leave their parishes.[5] Nearly three thousand of them, including a number of eminent men, — for under Edward some Puritan ministers had been appointed to bishoprics or other high offices, — were deposed,[6] and more than eight hundred fled out of England for their lives.[7] The pulpits of all Puritans were ordered to be closed, and two hundred and seventy-seven,[8] including some women and even some children, is the lowest estimate of the number of those put to death for their faith during the five years of her reign. Most of these victims were burned at the stake.

When Queen Elizabeth (1558-1603) succeeded Mary, the Protestants at first took courage. Her history and her supposed character seemed to assure them fair dealing at the least. But their hopes soon were dashed. In some respects her long reign was one of the most glorious in the history of England or of the world, but the treatment which her Protestant subjects received is a shameful stain upon its record. Historians still are undecided whether she personally were a Roman Catholic or not.[9] Apparently she was influenced more by political considerations than by any ecclesiastical or religious convictions.[10] She was nominally a Protestant and certainly was one so far as refusing formal allegiance to the Pope is concerned. Yet she often allowed her Protestant subjects to be treated worse than any others, although they took the oath of supremacy which the Romanists refused to take.[11] Many laws were equally severe in letter against both Romanists and Puritans, but she claimed the right to dictate as to their enforcement and more often, indeed almost uniformly, was bitterly harsh towards the Puritans. She did not hesitate to put a stop to legislation intended for their relief,[12] and the infamous Star Chamber and Court of High Commission were allowed to pursue their cruel work steadily.

It is worth while to notice some of the particular grievances of the Puritans. For one thing, absolute uniformity in religious observances was insisted upon.[13] Not the slightest liberty was permitted under any circumstances. For example, no portion of Scripture except that prescribed could be read at public worship, whether that happened to be appropriate to the occasion or not.[14] Furthermore, this uniformity was not confined to matters of ritual but included even the costume of the clergy.[15] The Puritans did not object to a dress distinctive of the clerical profession, but the garb which their ministers, like others, were obliged by law to wear was associated so closely with Popery in their minds that they abhorred it. A fine of twenty pounds a month was proclaimed for absence from the parish church.[16] Even persons who attended church regularly on Sundays, if they also met in private at home for religious conversation and Scripture reading upon holidays, when many evil practices were common, were punishable for that.[17] Clergymen themselves actually were forbidden to join in observing days of personal fasting and prayer for the queen and the Church.[18]

Spies were appointed in every parish in which there were suspected persons, so that offenders might be denounced.[19] All Puritan publications were forbidden and sometimes, when discovered, were publicly burned, and if the printers were detected, their presses were destroyed.[20] Worst of all, not only were a multitude of clergymen in sympathy with Protestantism deposed, but men ignorant and even known to be depraved were appointed to fill their places. About 1571 the House of Commons itself declared in a formal address to the queen that "for lack of true discipline in the Church great numbers are admitted ministers that are infamous in their lives,"[21] and in a petition to Parliament for relief in 1586 the Puritan ministers asserted that "the bishops have made priests of the basest of the people, not only for their occupations and trades whence they have taken them, as shoemakers, barbers, tailors, water-bearers, shepherds, and horse-keepers, but also for their want of good learning and honesty."[22] Among the clergy in office there was such a dearth of even intellectual fitness that for some time there was no one in so large a town as Northampton who could preach a sermon, nor was there one in the whole county of Cornwall;[23] and a similar, although not so extreme, lack existed in London itself.[24] Certainly the Church was in a bad way. Yet even this is not the whole story. In spite of the unhallowed license in instituting new clergymen, not enough of them, such as they were, were appointed to minister to the people. Scores of parishes remained vacant.[25] Now and then there actually was no minister available to bury the dead.[26]

Naturally such a condition of affairs could have but one result. Large numbers of the people became practically heathen. Yet the authorities both civil and ecclesiastical applied almost their whole strength to the work of eradicating Puritanism and took little or no notice of the prevailing corruption of society.[27] Of course the Puritans appealed for relief repeatedly to the ecclesiastical powers, to Parliament and to the queen, but seldom with any success. Those who were disposed to relieve them were too few and had too little power. Such was their condition under Queen Elizabeth. As for the reign of King James I (1603–25), it only needs to be said that he continued in general the same policy of oppression. He declared that the Puritans were "insufferable in any well-governed commonwealth" and that he would "make them conform" or "harry them out of the land or else worse."[28]

This historical outline indicates how intolerable the condition of the English Puritans was during the larger portion of the two centuries before the Pilgrims abandoned their native land. Christians who conscientiously disagreed with the doctrines or practices of the State Church were compelled to acquiesce in a generally prevalent condition of grave moral evil and also to submit to religious intolerance and civil persecution of the most unjust and often the most cruel sort, or else fly the country. It requires no vivid fancy to conceive of their sufferings in detail, and the most active imagination hardly can overdraw the picture. It is not to be asserted that none of the Puritans themselves were indiscreet, needlessly regardless of law, or otherwise open to just criticism. Some of them were at this period; and later, when Puritanism had won control of England for a time, it exhibited too much of the same intolerance from which it formerly had suffered. But, for the most part, this was not until long after the Pilgrims had emigrated.

Up to the time of their departure the Puritans, to speak with restraint, were as intelligent, orderly, devout, patriotic, and useful citizens as could be found in the whole land. It was the divine purpose that, when the time for the transplanting of Protestantism to the New World should come, representatives of the best ability and purest Christianity in England should be prepared to undertake the task.

CHAPTER II.

PURITANISM AND CONGREGATIONALISM.

THE Pilgrims were Puritans, but they were more than merely Puritans. They were also Congregationalists. Modern Christians who bear this name are their direct ecclesiastical descendants and the glory of their heroism is our legitimate inheritance. It is important, therefore, to examine the process by which Congregationalism grew out of Puritanism.

The outcome of the tyranny with which the Puritans were treated was what might have been expected. "The blood of the martyrs is the seed of the Church." History abounds in illustrations of this truth, and scarcely any other is more striking than that afforded by the Pilgrims. Oppression always confirms many of its objects in their beliefs and provokes them to a more or less open resistance. Partly for this general reason and partly because similar religious persecutions on the continent, as well as the demands of English trade, had led many Protestant French, Germans, and Dutch to settle in England, especially in the eastern counties,[1] Puritan opinions spread steadily in certain portions of the kingdom during the latter half of the sixteenth century. It seems to be the fact that these foreign immigrants, many of whom had been not only permitted but even invited to establish themselves in England because of their skill in manufacturing, were treated much less rigorously than the native Protestants and, in some instances at least, were allowed to maintain their own churches,[2] and their example and influence cannot have failed to promote the growth of Puritanism among the English themselves.

Thus there came to be three distinct religious parties in the realm. One was the Anglican, or Established Church, composed of the conforming Protestants. This often was more Romish than Protestant in practice, although no longer acknowledging the Pope as its head. A second was composed of the actual Roman Catholics. They were always active, and, although persecuted sharply now and then when any of their frequent and treasonable plots had come to light, they ordinarily were permitted a well-understood although legally prohibited existence. The third party was composed of the Puritans, or non-conforming Protestants, many of whom also were called Separatists.

The first regular Puritan congregations on record seem to have met in and around London about 1553.[3] Certainly one numbering two hundred then was formed in that city, meeting wherever it could avoid discovery. But, apparently in 1557, it was detected at Islington, and its minister, Mr. Rough, and a deacon,

Mr. Simpson, were burned at the stake.[4] About 1566, however, it reassembled in London and adopted the Genevan service book.[5] This was its formal separation from the Church of England and the beginning of organized Presbyterianism in that country. Congregations gradually were formed afterwards in Suffolk, Essex, Warwickshire, Northamptonshire, and elsewhere. The writings of Calvin began to be introduced into the country and to be studied by many of the ministers, and Puritanism soon grew apace, although never free, except temporarily in certain localities, from the active hostility of the public authorities, both ecclesiastical and civil. The persecution which already has been described was maintained constantly and energetically.

At this point the more important subjects of difference between the adherents of the Established Church and the Puritans should be mentioned.[6] The former, although repudiating for themselves the authority of the Pope, held that the Papal Church is a true church of God. The latter disputed this. The former insisted upon the spiritual as well as the legal supremacy of the crown and its magistrates. The later conceded the legal but denied the spiritual supremacy. The former asserted the authority of bishops over the presbyters, or ordinary clergy. The latter declared that bishops ought to be regarded merely as presidents of boards of presbyters and as having no right of ruling except with the free concurrence of the presbyters. The former claimed that certain titles, offices, and usages of their Church, — such as the titles and offices of archdeacons, deans, and others, and the usages of making the sign of the cross in baptism, singing prayers, etc., — which had been constituted or adopted during the centuries subsequent to the age of the apostles, are equally genuine or authoritative with those instituted by the apostles themselves. The latter insisted upon the primitive apostolic titles and forms, as they understood them, as the only true ones.

The Puritans also were opposed to set and formal prayers, unless some liberty of extemporaneous petition were allowed, and to the reading of the apocryphal books of the Bible in public worship, especially as portions of the accepted canon of the Scriptures were omitted. They were unwilling to observe saints' days and certain Church festival occasions, and believed the practice of fasting on Friday and in Lent to have no Biblical warrant. They also contended that access to the sacrament was much too freely allowed in the Established Church, and that discipline should be maintained and care taken to prohibit persons of unworthy life from the communion. Moreover, as has been said already, although not objecting to a distinctively clerical dress in itself, they repudiated all costumes resembling those worn by Roman Catholic priests. On these, as on some minor matters, the differences between them and the Established Church were radical. It is worthy of remark in passing that these differences related almost wholly to questions of practice rather than of doctrine. But the attitude of the Puritans toward them was based upon principle and was uncompromising.

The Puritanism which has thus been described was essentially Presbyterianism. It was an aristocratic system, not then fully developed, as at present, into its grades of presbyteries, synods, and assemblies, yet containing them all in essence and in prospect. Moreover, these Presbyterian Puritans merely wished to reform the Established Church, not to leave it.[7] There was to be another outcome of the Puritan movement, a more democratic and independent Christian body, the Congregationalists.

The recorded beginnings of Congrega-

Faith Monument.

tionalism occurred during the last quarter of the sixteenth century. The earliest Congregationalists, of whom Robert Browne was the pioneer, were earnest Puritans. They dissented stoutly from the Established Church. They agreed with the Presbyterian Puritans upon every one of the points of difference which have been mentioned. But they went beyond the Presbyterians themselves. They insisted upon the independence of each local church, and upon the divinely given right and duty of each church to govern itself democratically while maintaining a common and equal fellowship with every other church. They derived their positions from the teaching of the Scriptures and from the example of the apostolic churches.

These principles were first advocated by Robert Browne about 1580. Probably the earliest Congregational church was that to which he ministered in Norwich, apparently in that year.[8] But the first which established itself permanently seems to have been that formed in London in 1592,[9] although the same thing had been attempted there as early as 1587. By degrees other Congregational churches sprang up and the spread of their principles evidently was more rapid than would naturally be expected. In 1580 Sir Walter Raleigh said that he was afraid that there were "near twenty thousand Brownists"—which is the name by which Congregationalists were known at first for a while—"in England."[10] Undoubtedly this estimate must have been excessive because that year was the one in the course of which their characteristic views first began to be proclaimed. It is most improbable that they spread so rapidly. But the historian Neal states that these Brownists "increased and made a considerable figure towards the latter end" of Queen Elizabeth's reign,[11] and May also declares that "before the death of Elizabeth"—which occurred only thirteen years after their body began to exist — "they had spread themselves widely through the country."[12] There is no satisfactory evidence that any large number of churches were formed by them as early as this, but the popular mind must have been in an accessible and receptive condition for such teachings as theirs, and probably there came to be a considerable number of those who individually accepted the opinions of the Brownists.[13] In 1602 there was a Congregational church in Gainsborough, the fortunes of which will be alluded to again.

As the subject of this chapter is considered it is well to bear in mind that, speaking strictly, there was a distinction between Puritanism and mere Separatism, or Nonconformity. Not all Puritans were Separatists, because some Puritans wished to remain in the State Church and reform it. Nor were all Separatists Puritans. The Roman Catholics were Separatists as truly as any of the Puritans, because they also refused to conform to the Established Church. Nevertheless the Separatists often are spoken of synonymously with the Puritans. The latter were more hostile to the Roman Catholic than they were to the Established Church, and their Nonconformity was so unlike that of the Roman Catholics that the two bodies rarely, if ever, are included together under the title which really covers them both.

No such distinction existed at first between Puritanism and Presbyterianism, but they did not long remain identical. Out of Presbyterian Puritanism grew the simpler and — as millions of Christians still believe[14] — purer and more apostolic Congregationalism. Doubtless there were then, as there are now, true Christians in every branch of the Church on earth, even the most corrupt. But the history of those who at this time revived what they believed to be the original Congregationalism will be found, as the study of it is pursued, to be a record of intelligent, patient, energetic, and fruitful loyalty to Christ which, it is safe to say, never has been surpassed, and which ever since their time has been of great and honorable service to mankind.

CHAPTER III.

ROBERT BROWNE.

THE history of any great social or religious movement is largely that of its individual leaders. It is necessary, therefore, to examine their careers closely, and such study always has a peculiar interest. It has been said already that Robert Browne was the pioneer of Congregationalism, and this chapter shall be devoted to him.[1] He has been ardently admired and commended by some writers and vigorously condemned and even abused by others. The truth about him seems to lie between the two extremes. His career certainly was striking and picturesque, in some respects most honorable and in others undeniably discreditable. So many facts now have become known about him that it is quite possible at last to form a comparatively impartial estimate of what he was and what he did.

He was born at Tolethorpe, in Rutlandshire, about 1550. He was of gentle blood, and his family was influential. Little is known concerning his childhood, but in 1570 he entered Corpus Christi, or Benet, College at Cambridge, and apparently he took his degree in due course as Bachelor of Arts. ' Yet there is some confusion about this part of his life because he also is said to have been chaplain in the family of the Duke of Norfolk in 1571, which appears to be a fact, yet which ordinarily would not be true of an undergraduate student. Even as early as this he must have come under Puritan influences, for he was charged with uttering seditious religious doctrines. For the next few years he probably taught school in Southwark, a part of London, speaking occasionally on Sundays to Puritan congregations gathered in a gravel pit in Islington, near at hand, and thereby he incurred the hostility of the ecclesiastical authorities. Evidently he was looking forward to becoming a preacher and was learning to exercise his gifts.

But the plague broke out and of course interfered with both schools and public worship and he returned home, probably in 1578. Next, and soon, he reappeared in Cambridge and became a theological student with Rev. Richard Greenham, of Dry Drayton close by, and, beginning to preach, he proved very acceptable to his hearers. He must have shown conspicuous ability, for in spite of the distrust of some of the ecclesiastics, who probably were acquainted with his history and more than suspected him of inclining towards Puritanism, he was invited to a pulpit in Cambridge itself, an unusual honor for so young a man. This invitation, however, he declined. Evidently his Puritan convictions were gaining strength, for he now began to preach boldly against the authority of the bishops, and soon, during a serious illness which befell him, the bishop and council of the diocese prohibited him formally from further preaching, which of course cut off his opportunities. Thus far his career had been that of a devout, well-educated, eloquent, and perhaps brilliant, but also impetuous and probably sometimes rash young man.

Upon his recovery he learned that in Norfolk there were people who sympathized more or less fully with his Puritan beliefs, and therefore that region appeared to promise more liberty of thought and a better opportunity for congenial labor than others. So he removed to Norwich and went to live with Robert Harrison, a friend who held views much like his own. Probably the reason why an exceptional religious freedom seemed possible there is that Norwich contained many of the foreign immigrants inclined toward Protestantism who have been mentioned already.[2] But Browne was not content to accept his religious views ready-made.

He was an independent and fearless student and he soon passed beyond the limits of the Presbyterianism with which up to that time Puritanism had been identical. He thought out afresh and restated, with the Scriptures for his guide, the original, apostolical Congregational system. Here too, in 1580 or 1581, apparently the former year, he organized and became pastor of the first purely and formally established Congregational church on record in England.

The authorities, however, had no idea of allowing such a system to be promulgated even in Norwich. His boldness soon gained for him their active hostility, and after several remonstrances, to which he paid no heed and from the severer consequences of which he was saved only by the mediation of his relative, Lord Treasurer Burghley, he and most of his followers emigrated in a body to Middleburg, in Zeland. Those who remained in Norwich sustained the church there for twenty-five years longer, if not more; but its subsequent history is obscure. Probably it died, and certainly it does not seem to have been the direct ancestor of any church now existing in that place. Browne and his company stayed in Middleburg two years, in the course of which he had three treatises printed, which were circulated in England and which were deemed so revolutionary, at least in an ecclesiastical sense, that the queen issued a special proclamation against them, and two men, John Copping and Elias Thacker, of whom we shall hear again, were hanged for distributing them.

Such a man as Browne was, however, often is hard to live with, and the inevitable conditions of exile doubtless embarrassed the little church of the emigrants. At any rate, internal troubles soon began to annoy it and Browne resigned its pastorate on three occasions, withdrawing his resignation each time by general request, which indicates that whatever blame existed did not lie specially with him. But at last, about the end of the year 1583, he sailed for Scotland with four or five families of his adherents. Here he passed some six months traveling, writing, preaching, and disputing. His life from youth on for a number of years, perhaps necessarily because of the unpopularity of his convictions, was largely one of controversy. The Edinburgh Presbytery, under the recognized authority of which he must have come in some manner, tried him for heresy, but he escaped conviction, and he soon went back to London, apparently feeble in body and discouraged in spirit.

He seems to have been imprisoned for a time but to have been released through Lord Treasurer Burghley's renewed intercession and to have been put in charge of his father at Stamford. It is declared, but not established, that his father disowned him, and it appears to be true that his courage and zeal revived for a while so far that he resumed his obnoxious preaching, this time at Northampton. But the end of his career as a Separatist soon came. It is remarkable that apparently, in spite of his pronounced Separatist and Congregationalist opinions, he never had formally severed his early connection with the Established Church. Probably he never had taken the trouble to do this, assuming that he practically had seceded from it in pursuing his chosen course so persistently, and had left the Established Church to expel him if it had cared to do so, as it had not. At any rate it is clear that both it and he now recognized the fact that he never had separated himself or had been separated from it formally, or there would have been little or no significance in what at this juncture plainly was a vital matter to him — the fact that he now was excommunicated for contempt by the bishop of Peterborough, in whose diocese he found himself.

This was the finishing blow to his Nonconformity. Worn out, despairing of the spread of his opinions, and doubtless importuned persistently by his relatives and many of his friends, and perhaps even honestly persuaded that he had been mistaken hitherto, he yielded, was readmitted to the Established Church, and was made master of St. Olave's grammar school in Southwark. In 1591 he became rector of the small parish of Achurch-cum-Thorpe in the diocese of Peterborough, and there he spent the remainder of his life, more than forty years.

Accounts are vague and various about his character and usefulness during this portion of his career, but it is certain that he never attained further distinction and he appears to have attracted no more special notice. He had spent his energies during his earlier years in what must have come to seem to him a fruitless and hopeless battle for the truth, and he went back into the Established Church, however sincerely, a broken man, too heavily burdened with the consciousness of defeat ever to accomplish much more of importance. It is reported that he died at last in Northampton jail, where he had been put for striking a constable who had been rude to him in his old age.

It is only natural that both Church of England and Puritan writers should have expressed themselves with severity about him. Of course the former have condemned him for adopting Separatist views at all and the latter for his final repudiation of them. But it is probable that he has been censured unduly. He must have possessed a nervous temperament and a weak physical constitution, and certainly he experienced extreme and enfeebling sufferings. He once declared that he had been imprisoned in thirty-two different dungeons, in some of which he could not see his own hand at noonday. He undeniably was eccentric, and the theory that during the latter half of his life he was at least partially insane has reasonable and considerable support. There is good evidence also that up to middle age he was not only exemplary in life but also was a clear-headed and able thinker and a man who won and retained the confidence and esteem of many good men. The history of his life is sad but not necessarily as discreditable as sometimes has been claimed.

At any rate the value of his services as the rediscoverer of Congregationalist principles cannot be denied successfully. He wrote eight books, of which three now are accessible. They are called, respectively, *A True and Short Declaration, etc.; A Treatise of Reformation Without Tarrying for Any, etc.*, which contains three distinct treatises, of which the third, entitled *A Book which sheweth the life and manners of all true Christians, etc.*, often is quoted; and *An Answer to Master Cartwright, His Letter for Joining with the English Churches, etc.* From these the principles which he taught are easily gleaned. They are in substance as follows : —

1. It is the first duty of each Christian to attain the highest possible purity of faith and life.

2. The corruption of the Church of England and its subjection to an unscriptural hierarchy should lead every true Christian at once to try to reform it.

3. There is no hope of this reform through the civil power.

4. Nor through Presbyterianism.

5. Therefore true believers should abandon the State church and form separate companies.

6. Any such company, if rightly associated, is a true church of Christ and is independent of all control except His.

7. The organization of such a church is by the voluntary and public adoption of a covenant with God and one another, this covenant being sealed by the sacrament of baptism.

8. Church government consists in the supreme lordship of Christ, each individual Christian being a regent of Christ equally with every other.

9. The ordinary officers of such a church, according to the Scriptures, are a pastor, or preacher; a teacher, or instructor; one or more elders, or advisers; one or more relievers, to supervise charities; and one or more widows, to care for the sick or distressed.

10. The sacrament of the Lord's Supper is the

seal of the mutual union of the members of such a church and of their union with Christ.

11. Mutual spiritual oversight and care are duties.

12. The fellowship of such churches is to be maintained, yet in harmony with the independence of each separate church.

This system is not only essential but also almost exact Congregationalism as it is practiced at present. But its office of teacher now usually is combined with that of pastor, and its elders have become deacons and also attend to much of the work of the relievers and widows, although in most modern churches there are devout women who unofficially perform this sort of service, and in some churches definitely appointed deaconesses take charge of it.

It is clear, therefore, that, in spite of whatever may have been subject for regret and even condemnation in Browne's career, there was much which was praiseworthy and of permanent value to the world. If he merited considerable blame, he also deserved sincere pity and some admiration. At any rate he is entitled fairly to the credit of having been the pioneer Congregationalist of his own and the succeeding generations.

CHAPTER IV.

CONGREGATIONAL PUBLICATIONS AND MARTYRS.

IT has been stated already that during the fifteenth and sixteenth centuries scores and even hundreds of Puritans were put to death for their faith. Many more also were martyred quite as truly by being caused to languish in the loathsome prisons of that day until they died there. The names of a number of such victims are recorded. Those of others long have been forgotten upon earth. But, although unquestionably it was a relief to many, for whom no hope of release remained, to be taken from the horrors of prison life to execution, one and all were martyrs in the truest sense. Congregationalism, as such, was represented among them, and the names of at least six men, who were killed before the year 1600, are known.

Before mentioning them, however, it is desirable to notice briefly certain publications which had great influence in extending and intensifying that revolt against the Established Church which was punished so severely. Their claim upon our attention lies in the fact that they probably were written in large part, if not altogether, by Congregationalists. A number of preliminary publications had prepared the way for them. Thomas Cartwright,[1] for example, wrote several treatises between 1572 and 1593 urging Presbyterian views and was imprisoned once for so doing. He held to the theory of a State church with a Presbyterian organization. He was not a Congregationalist and, more than any one else, is credited with having given English Puritanism in its Presbyterian character a definite form. A number of other publications antagonizing the Established Church, some written at home and others on the Continent, also were circulated in England at about this period,[2] often anonymously because of the risk of acknowledged authorship.

They and the many replies to them all helped to arouse the popular mind, and it is difficult for modern readers to appreciate the strength of the public feeling in regard to the subject which in different forms and manners they discussed. The daily dissemination of news of all sorts, to which we are accustomed through the telegraph and the press, was then unknown. People had comparatively few subjects about which to talk, and therefore those which they did have were apt to be discussed with the more earnestness. Moreover, their religious and ecclesiastical differences probably existed more or less sharply almost everywhere throughout the kingdom, and the universal consciousness of the vital importance of spiritual matters, from which even careless minds cannot wholly escape, must have added intensity to the situation.

Such being the condition of affairs,

there appeared late in the year 1588 the first of the treatises specially under our notice, the famous Martin Mar-Prelate tracts. It was entitled *Oh Read ouer D. Iohn Bridges, etc.*, and, at least nominally, was a reply to a work by Dr. Bridges, the Dean of Sarum, in defense of the Church of England. In the course of about seven months six other such tracts came out.[3] The author never has been identified positively. John Penry seems to have published them and he generally has been believed their author. But recently it has been argued, and with much force, that probably they were from the pen of Henry Barrowe.[4] They are terse, colloquial, fiery, and satirical. But for the justice of their charges they might be called abusive. They are boldly personal and defiantly severe. They were caught up eagerly and read widely. They caused the people to laugh and the ecclesiastics to stand aghast, and they made a profound and lasting impression. They provoked several replies in the same vein, roused the authorities to a fury of indignation, and occasioned fresh persecutions quite as harsh as any before. One result was the martyrdom of several of the six Congregationalists now to be mentioned.

Of three of the six very little is known. One was John Copping,[5] already alluded to, of Bury St. Edmunds, who perhaps was a minister, but more probably was a layman. He was imprisoned from 1576 to 1583 for disregarding certain ecclesiastical laws. He was tried repeatedly but refused to recant and managed somehow, even while in jail, to circulate actively the writings of Robert Browne and Robert Harrison. Finally he was hanged for these offenses at Bury on June 5, 1583. Another, Elias Thacker,[6] was Copping's fellow prisoner for most of the time, held the same beliefs and shared his labors as a disseminator of Congregationalist principles, was condemned at the same time and was hanged the day before

Copping at the same place.[7] The third, William Dennis,[8] is known to posterity in respect to his character only through the single statement afterward made by Governor Bradford, of the Plymouth Colony, that "he was a godly man and faithful in his place."[9] He, too, was executed publicly as a Separatist. Brief although these records are, they are now like crowns of glory upon the heads of the men to whom they relate.

Of the other three fortunately we know more. Greenwood, Barrowe, and Penry are historic and honored names in the long and noble story of English Nonconformity. John Greenwood[10] was a Cambridge graduate in 1580–81, who became a clergyman of the State Church, but later was domestic chaplain to Lord Robert Rich, of Rochford, Essex, an eminent Puritan. He abandoned the Established Church and was arrested in London, in 1586, for holding a religious service in a private house. He was confined in the

Clink Prison, and here he wrote two treatises which he managed to have printed. In 1592, he was released on bail for a time and helped in September to organize the first Congregational church in London, taking the office of teacher, Francis Johnson being pastor; but early in December, the news having reached the authorities, he was reconfined. During most of his imprisonment he had as a fellow prisoner Henry Barrowe,[11] already mentioned as perhaps the real Martin Mar-Prelate.

Barrowe was a native of Shipdam, Norfolk, a graduate of Cambridge, a lawyer at Gray's Inn, a courtier, and for a time, according to Lord Bacon, a man of dissolute life. Converted by hearing a single sermon, he became interested in theology and church government and identified himself with the Congregationalists in the effort to secure reform. He was arrested November 19, 1586, without a warrant, while visiting Greenwood in the Clink

Prison, and was kept in jail there during most, if not all, of the remainder of his life. He managed to write and secure the publication of at least six books of his own as well as four others written in conjunction with Greenwood. It is a marvel, yet a fact, that, in spite of the vigilance of the authorities, these two men, while in prison, contrived to compose twelve able volumes and to get them smuggled, doubtless piecemeal, out of jail and then surreptitiously printed. How they managed to do this we can only imagine. It must have been by the aid of friendly visitors who succeeded in baffling the scrutiny of the watchful jailers. The zeal and determination of the reformers could not have been demonstrated more conclusively. Barrowe appears to have possessed the more original and controlling mind and to have chiefly shaped their common utterances. He advocated a distinct and peculiar theory of Congregationalism, now known as Barrowism, in which there was a considerable and an unnatural mixture of Presbyterianism. Barrowe, with Greenwood, was tried several times, made able arguments which proved very troublesome to the authorities, and finally, after a reprieve or two, both of the friends were alleged to be guilty of having declared the queen to be unbaptized, the state so corrupt that no Christians could live in it peaceably, and all the people infidels. Such extravagant charges carry their own refutations on their faces. Nevertheless, the two men were hanged on April 6, 1593.

The sixth of these martyrs was John Penry,[12] a Welshman. He was a Roman Catholic in youth and graduated at Cambridge in 1583-84, where he had become a Puritan. He then went to Oxford and gained the degree of Master of Arts. Later he took holy orders and earned a good repute as a scholar and preacher. In 1587 he wrote and printed a vigorous appeal for better preaching in Wales. He soon became active in publishing secretly the writings of the various Puritan authors, notably the Martin Mar-Prelate tracts, and had to fly for safety in 1589 to Scotland, but in 1592 he was back in London and was one of the newly formed Congregational church. He was arrested March 22, 1593, and imprisoned. The contemptible meanness of the authorities is shown by the fact that he was tried for only having begun privately to compose a petition to the queen, which never was sent, or even completed, but which was discovered to contain an appeal for liberty of worship. He was convicted and on May 29 he was put to death, doubtless like the others, by being hanged.

It is not probable that even the ecclesiastical authorities perceived clearly, if at all, the distinction between these men and the other Puritans who had been slain for the faith. To the rulers the then hardly more than suggested differences between Presbyterian and Congregational Puritanism must have been too insignificant for notice. Probably their condemnation appeared, even to their companions and to the martyrs themselves, to be due, and was due, to the general fact rather than to the particular method of their dissent from the State Church. Nevertheless they were genuine Congregationalist martyrs, of whom all modern members of that branch of Christ's Church, who are their spiritual descendants and who bear their likeness more or less closely, never should cease to be tenderly proud. How it would have comforted them if they could have foreseen that the utterly improbable would become actual, that the truths for which they died would find wide and loyal acceptance among men, and that, three centuries later, the anniversaries of the martyrdom of some of them would be celebrated with reverent affection and honor by English Congregationalists in the very London and on the same spot where they yielded up their lives ! [13]

CHAPTER V.

SCROOBY AND AUSTERFIELD.

WE now are prepared to consider the Pilgrims themselves, and it will be pleasant to form some idea at this point of the region which was the English home of many among them. It has been said already that in 1602 there was a Congregational church in Gainsborough-upon-Trent, in Lincolnshire. John Smyth was its pastor. In 1606,[1] doubtless because of persecution, its majority headed by Mr. Smyth emigrated to Amsterdam. Some and probably most of the remainder lived in or near to Scrooby, in Nottinghamshire, a few miles to the westward, the village now famous as the place where the Pilgrim movement first took definite form. The modern Scrooby, identical in site with the ancient, lies on the Great Northern Railroad about a hundred and fifty miles nearly north of London, fifty miles west from the North Sea near Grimsby, and ninety miles east from Liverpool. It is perhaps eight or ten miles south of Doncaster. The old turnpike road from London to York and Scotland passes through it. Probably its population is not over one hundred and fifty persons at present and it hardly can have been much larger three centuries ago.

Looking west from the platform of the railway station, one sees, not more than a thousand feet distant, a cluster of low cottages, chiefly of brick, with tiled or thatched roofs, and shaded by overhanging elms. Hedges border most of the narrow lanes and in the midst of the cottages lies the ancient graveyard in which stands the parish church, St. Wilfred's. This has been restored and also enlarged by adding an aisle upon the south side since the time of the Pilgrims, but its graceful spire remains the same as then. In the eastern distance low hills form the horizon, and woods limit the view more narrowly towards the west. The neighborhood, although not level, hardly undulates enough to be called hilly, and consists of cultivated fields or green meadows, separated by hedges and dotted with elms, which shade the grazing cattle. It is a quiet farming region, not picturesque but possessing in a high degree that charm of peacefulness so characteristic of much English scenery.

Walking up the lane from the railway to the village, one sees at once upon his right hand an irregular meadow containing perhaps six acres and separated from the lane by a fence and a ditch. Beyond the meadow is a farmhouse, long and narrow, extending north and south, having two stories and an attic, with walls partly of brick and partly of rubble or rough plaster of some kind, and with low outbuildings on the east side and a garden, barnyards, and barns and sheds on the west.

The whole estate doubtless is much smaller than it was formerly, but in 1867 it still included about seventy acres. One of its most conspicuous features at present is a short row of Lombardy poplars along the wall on the brink of the Ryton, the little river which forms the northern border of the garden. This house stands in part upon the site of the ancient manor-house. To reach it one must pass around through the edge of the village and across the meadow. At first glance it exhibits no appearance of noteworthy antiquity, but examination discovers in its western wall, near the southern end on the outside, a wide, high arch, sunken in the surface of the building, and a deep and peculiar niche, neither of which has any modern use or meaning. The wall of this part of the house is very thick, like those customarily built in great houses in England three or four hundred years ago, and the shape and arrangement of some rooms in this portion of the structure testify to their great age.

There is much probability that this part of the building was included in the original manor-house.

The estate belonged to the archbishopric of York and was used for occasional retirement and as a resting-place in journeying to or from London. It was pleasant and also comparatively secluded, although easily accessible. Margaret, Queen of Scotland, daughter of Henry VII, slept there on her way to Scotland. Henry VIII lodged there at least once, Hunter, the eminent English antiquary, says on June 12, 1543,[2] and James I liked it so much that he tried, but in vain, to buy it.[3] The original house must have been built before the year 1500, for at that date Archbishop Savage spent a large sum upon it.[4] Hunter adds that the same archbishop "often made this his place of residence for the purpose of hunting in Hatfield chase."[5] The historian Leland says that in 1541 it was

a great manor-place standinge withyn a mote and

[be]longing to the Archbishop of York: builded yn [in] to [two] courtes, whereof the first is very ample, and all builded of tymbre, saving the front of the haule, that is of bricke, to the wych *ascenditur per gradus lapidis* [ascent is made by stone steps]. The ynner courte building, as far as I marked, was of tymbre building, and was not in compace past the 4 [quarter] parte of the utter [outer] courte.[6]

In 1557 Archbishop Heath leased the estate for twenty-one years at £20 15s. per year to his steward, James Bryne. In 1575 Archbishop Grindal leased it on the same terms to William Marshall. Later, in December, 1582, Archbishop Sandys leased it to his oldest son, Sir Samuel, for £65 6s. 8d., and he leased it, probably, to William Brewster's father and, certainly, to William Brewster himself after the senior Brewster's death.[7] We know that William Brewster, the Pilgrim, lived there from April 1, 1594, to September 30, 1607.[8]

In addition to the protecting moat the house had ornamental and useful fishponds and gardens, and unquestionably it was for the times a stately and imposing edifice. After having been leased to successive tenants for a generation or two it was mostly taken down, and probably before the middle of the seventeenth century, for Thoroton in 1673 spoke of it as having been standing "within memory." Probably a farmhouse was built upon a part of its site at once. At present the location of the courts and the plan of the building and its grounds remain conjectural. In 1871, by permission of the lord of the manor, the late Lord Houghton, Dr. Henry M. Dexter, assisted by the writer, made many measurements and some excavations in the hope of determining these particulars. The meadow is full of remnants of masonry beneath the turf, and a few ridges and hollows indicate a possible outline. But no trustworthy conclusions can be formed unless after a more systematic and extended examination. Such details probably were recorded formerly and in full in the official documents of the archbishopric of York, but the most diligent search has failed to find them and it is evident that they have been lost or destroyed.

In the stone wall which extends from the rear of the house back to the river Ryton close by are broken pieces of chiseled stone which suggest the former stateliness of the building, and in two of the present cow-sheds the roofs are upheld by carved beams, the dimensions of which indicate that they once performed a similar service in the manor-house hall or chapel. Until recently — it is now reported to have disappeared — there remained in the garden a very old stump of a mulberry tree, said to have been planted by Cardinal Wolsey while dwelling at the manor for several weeks on his way to York after his fall from power.[9] The ditch along the south edge of the meadow also marks the line of that part of the original moat. These are the only visible traces of the early appearance of the place which remain. Its intimate connection with the history of the Pilgrims had been overlooked during the intervening centuries until in the summer of 1851 it was sought out by Dr. Dexter and at about the same time by Mr. George Sumner. Their published accounts of their observations directed attention to it afresh, and ever since it has been visited frequently, especially by Americans. At the close of the first International Congregational Council, held in London in July, 1891, that assembly made an expedition thither in a body and held an appropriate memorial service in the grounds.[10]

North of Scrooby about a mile lies the small market town, Bawtry, but, beyond the fact that probably some thus far unidentified Pilgrims lived there, it has no special claim upon our notice. Another mile, almost due north, brings one to Austerfield, a little hamlet smaller than

Scrooby and equally quiet. It contains a cottage in which, according to a tradition generally believed to possess some probability, William Bradford, the governor of the Plymouth Colony, was born, and it is a matter of record that he was baptized by Rev. Henry Fletcher on March 19, 1589, in its quaint little church, St. Helen's. Here he doubtless worshiped during his boyhood. This church, too, has been modernized somewhat within, but its low, rough buttressed walls of stone, its tiny belfry, its narrow windows with their diamond-shaped panes, its oak chancel rail, the Norman arch of its porch with its "zigzag and beak" ornamentation and its rude carving of a dragon, and the rough stone benches on either side of the porch, must be essentially as they have been from the first.

These are but few and disconnected links to bind the present to the past. Yet, when it is remembered that — except by the building of the railroad — the

BRADFORD COTTAGE, AUSTERFIELD.

region has undergone almost no change, that the fields and meadows lie substantially as they always have lain, that the courses of the highroad and most of the crossroads are essentially unaltered, that the tranquil waters of the Idle and the Ryton flowed formerly just where they flow to-day, and that the same shadowy hills bounded the horizon to the east and similar stretches of woodland to the west, it is easy to appreciate quite well how these scenes must have appeared to the familiar eyes of Brewster, Bradford, Robinson, and the others who helped to form the Pilgrim church.

CHAPTER VI.

WILLIAM BREWSTER AND
WILLIAM BRADFORD.

IT is a common belief that most of the Pilgrims who settled at Plymouth were from Scrooby or its vicinity originally. But some of the original emigrants from Scrooby never reached America, and the Plymouth colony included many who joined the Pilgrims in Holland, from different parts of England, as well as others who united with them first in England on their way hither. It is remarkable and to be regretted that so little is known of the Pilgrims personally, especially of the members of the Scrooby church. But fortunately something is recorded about several concerning whom information is most desirable.

One of these is William Brewster.[1]

Both for his personal qualities and as one of the foremost leaders of their undertaking, he always must remain a conspicuous figure in their history. Probably he was born in Scrooby about 1566. At any rate, his father, William, and his mother, Prudence, lived there, in the manor-house, in 1571, when he apparently was not more than four or five years old. He was matriculated at Peterhouse, Cambridge University, December 13, 1580, but it is unlikely that he took the full course. Bradford, the Pilgrim historian, says that he "spent some small time" there. Afterwards he found his way to London and to the royal court and entered the service of William Davison, Queen Elizabeth's secretary of state, and this fact is evidence of the good social position of his family.[2] Bradford relates that Davison

> found him so discreete and faithfull as he trusted him above all other that were aboute him, and only employed him in all matters of greatest trust and secrecie. He esteemed him rather as a sonne than

a servante, and for his wisdom and godlines (in private) he would converse with him more like a friend & familiar than a maister.³

At about this period England undertook to aid Holland in her conflict with Spain, and when Davison was sent as ambassador to the Low Countries in the Earl of Leicester's time there, among other purposes to receive charge of Flushing and Brill, which were given over temporarily to the English in 1585 as security for the performance by the Dutch of their new treaty obligations to Queen Elizabeth, the keys of Flushing, apparently the more important, were committed to Brewster, and he slept with them under his pillow at least one night. Later, when Davison, after returning to England, was deposed, being made a scapegoat for the queen in connection with the execution of Mary, Queen of Scots, Brewster withdrew from the court and soon went back to Scrooby. Here he held the position of agent of the Archbishop of York, the owner of the manor, and he also was government postmaster. This does not mean, however, that he kept a modern post office. Private letters were not carried by government until about thirty years later.[4] His duty was merely to forward official dispatches and occasional travelers. His office was one of honor and influence, appropriate for a gentleman by birth, and his salary was £90 to £100 a year, about the same sum then paid to a principal secretary of state,[5] a much larger sum, because of the greater value of money then, than it now seems. Davison was inclined to Puritanism, and association with him doubtless had helped to develop Separatist convictions in Brewster, and, after returning to Scrooby, Brewster took active interest in promoting the religious welfare of that part of England. But apparently he had not yet left the Established Church. Bradford says : —

> Afterwards he wente and lived in ye country, in good esteeme amongst his freinds and ye gentlemen of those parts, espetially the godly & religious.

He did much good in ye countrie wher he lived, in promoting and furthering religion, not only by his practiss & example, and provocking and incouraging of others, but by procuring of good preachers to ye places thereaboute, and drawing on of others to assist & help forward in such a worke; he himselfe most commonly deepest in ye charge, & sometimes above his abillitie.[6]

We can imagine easily and with reasonable accuracy the life which he led at this time — that of a grave, dignified, devout, public-spirited country gentleman, busy with the cares of his pleasant estate and his probably not burdensome official duties, and happy in the friendship of the choicest people of the vicinity. Yet he must have been distressed by his knowledge of the intolerance of the ecclesiastical authorities, and conscious of the unhappiness of his Separatist friends and of the increasing likelihood that loyalty to conscience soon must involve him in the same perils which threatened them.

When those members of the Gainsborough church who had been left behind by the emigration of their associates to Amsterdam established themselves at Scrooby, Brewster, by this time having become an avowed Separatist, was prominent among them, and as the manor-house contained a hall or chapel suitable for purposes of worship, and doubtless such as they could find nowhere else, his home became their headquarters. Moreover, his official position under government rendered them less likely to be detected or, if discovered, to be interfered with at first. Undoubtedly they organized their historic church under his roof. Bradford adds: —

> After they were joyned togither in communion, he was a spetial stay & help unto them. They ordinarily mett at his house on ye Lord's day (which was a manor of ye bishop's), and with great love he entertained them when they came, making provission for them to his great charge.[7]

When they determined at last to emigrate to Holland, Brewster had cast in his lot with them finally, and he acted as a leader in the undertaking and shared their gravest perils and sufferings. In Leyden he became the elder of the church. Having necessarily sacrificed much of his property in leaving England, he supported himself at first by teaching English and later by setting up a printing press, issuing especially Separatist books, which could not be printed in England; and he appears to have prospered, as was natural, more than most of the others.[8] In 1619 he was sent to London with Robert Cushman to negotiate in regard to the proposed emigration to America.[9] He was one of the Mayflower company and was accompanied by his wife, Mary, two sons, Love and Wrestling, and two servants, Richard More and his brother.[10] Another son, Jonathan, the eldest, came over in the Fortune in November, 1621.[11] Probably more than any other one person, except Governor Bradford, he was the mainstay of the feeble colony during the tedious and terrible years until its permanence and prosperity had become assured;

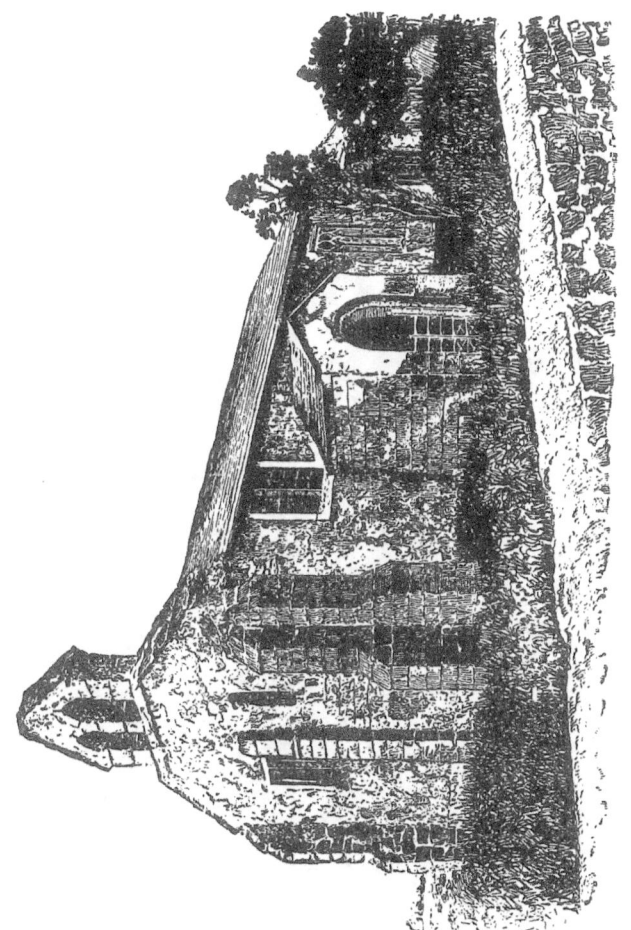

AUSTERFIELD CHURCH.

and the fact that he was seldom prominent in connection with the civil government is because, in the lack of a regular pastor, for nearly nine years he performed some of the duties of that office. He died on April 26, 1644.[12] He was a man of culture, travel, knowledge of the world, and diplomatic experience, as well as of thorough integrity and deep piety. In any age and any conditions he would have been a man of mark.

Another Pilgrim, something of whom is known, is William Bradford.[13] He was a native of Austerfield. As early as 1575 William Bradford and John Hanson appear to have been the two foremost men in the place. This Bradford had a son, William, and Hanson had a daughter, Alice. These two were married June 21, 1584, and became the parents of the future Pilgrim. The date of his birth is unknown, but probably it was early in 1589. It is recorded that Rev. Henry Fletcher baptized him in St. Helen's church, March

19, 1589. The Leyden records declare him to have been twenty-three in 1613, when he was married there on November 10, but they are the more likely to be inexact. When he was about two years old his father died, and his mother must have passed away soon after. When the orphaned lad was only about six he also lost his grandfather Bradford; and two uncles, Thomas and Richard Bradford, took charge of him. They attempted to make him a farmer. A severe illness early in his life developed serious convictions within him, and at about twelve years old the influence of the Bible and of Rev. Richard Clifton, for a short time the first pastor of the Scrooby church, impressed him strongly, and he soon became a Separatist and in time a member of the Pilgrim church.

He was only eighteen or nineteen when, with his religious companions, he emigrated to Holland. He inherited a little property, and Hunter says that his family seems to have been acquainted with the best people socially in the vicinity of Austerfield.[14] He had the tastes of a student and became somewhat accomplished as a linguist, philosopher, and theologian. He seems to have been a man of grave and modest demeanor, but of unusual versatility, good judgment, and executive capacity, and, especially in view of the conditions of his early life, of exceptional culture. In Leyden he, too, shared the common poverty of the company, and supported himself as a fustian worker. There, on December 10, 1613, he married Dorothy May, probably from Wisbeach, England, who was drowned in Cape Cod Bay, December 17, 1620. On August 24, 1623, at Plymouth in America, he married Mrs. Alice Southworth. There is a tradition that they had been lovers in their youth but had been separated by the influence of her parents. They had four children, John, William, Mercy, and Joseph. After the death of John Carver in April, 1621, he became governor of the colony, and this office he held, excepting during five years when his earnestly expressed desire to be relieved of the office was granted, until his death, which occurred May 19, 1657. He appears to have been the writer of the larger part of the record of the early experiences of the Pilgrims in New England known as *Mourt's Relation*, and his famous *History of Plymouth Plantations* is of intense interest as well as a standard source of information to all students of Pilgrim history. He also wrote three or four minor works.

These men, together with John Robinson, were the leaders of the Pilgrims, especially during the earliest years of their organic life. Brewster must have been about twenty years the older, and in many particulars the two were unlike, but there were marked resemblances between them apart from their common piety and purpose. Each supplemented the other effectively, and together they did a great work for humanity and for Christ.

CHAPTER VII.

JOHN ROBINSON.

FEW records of its kind would be prized more highly now than that of the organization of the Pilgrim church at Scrooby, if it were in existence. Perhaps there never was any upon paper. Even if such a document otherwise would have been felt to be necessary, the consequences of its possible capture by the ecclesiastical authorities would have been so ruinous to the church that, if there ever were one, it must have been carefully kept from public knowledge and doubtless it was lost or destroyed at last. We know where the church probably was formed, who its earliest pastor was, and the names of several of its lay members. But who else were included in it, how many there were in all, the precise date of its organization, and what simple ceremonies were observed upon the occasion — these facts never are likely to come to light.

The original pastor was Rev. Richard Clifton, who seems to have been a member of the church in Gainsborough before its division, already mentioned. Bradford calls him "a grave and reverēd preacher, who by his paines and diligens had done much good, and under God had ben a means of ye conversion of many."[1] But he soon became the teacher of the Scrooby church, John Robinson being chosen its pastor and evidently with Clifton's cordial assent, perhaps in part because of the latter's advanced years.[2] Up to the time of the departure of the Pilgrims from Holland to America, which will be described in due order, Robinson not only shared the preëminence of Brewster and Bradford in the company, but also in some respects was its chief member, and the veneration of all for his signal ability and exalted character endured unabated as long as any of them survived.

Robinson [3] probably was born at Gainsborough and about 1576. The registers of Leyden University record that he was thirty-nine when matriculated there on September 5, 1615. Hunter says that during the reign of Charles II certain Robinsons were prominent among the Separatists in Gainsborough,[4] and this fact may supply a clew to his origin. But his earliest appearance in the field of authentic history is upon joining Corpus Christi, or Benet, College at Cambridge when about seventeen. At this period Puritanism was so prevalent in Cambridge that its existence apparently had to be tolerated temporarily, and Robinson, probably already somewhat inclined in its favor, was attracted gradually to accept its principles. Nevertheless, after remaining in Cambridge seven years and distinguishing himself there sufficiently to be appointed to a fellowship belonging to his college, he took orders in the State Church and about 1600 he left Cambridge to enter upon work as a clergyman. For the next four years he labored in or near Norwich, probably as a curate.

Whether he went thither accidentally, or deliberately sought to go there because of its acknowledged sympathy with Puritanism, is unknown. In any case the spiritual atmosphere of the region, which had influenced Robert Browne and others so powerfully, soon affected him controllingly. His Separatist convictions gained strength by degrees and his expression of them became more frank, until at last his bishop, a sturdy foe of Puritanism, suspended him. Of course he could not officiate longer in Norwich, so about 1604 he left there, resigned his college fellowship, severed his connection with the Established Church, and went up to his home in the North, apparently joining the Congregational church in Gainsborough. When a part of this church soon afterwards accompanied its pastor, John Smyth, into exile at Amsterdam, Robinson went over to Scrooby with the remainder, and there he passed the short balance of his life in England as the successor of Clifton, in the pastorate of what became the Pilgrim church.

He must have assumed this office with a clear understanding of what it was likely to cost him. Persecution, swift and severe, was certain as soon as the action of his companions and himself should become known to their rulers, and it overtook them speedily. But by degrees and in spite of obstacles which only the profoundest faith and the stoutest courage could have overcome, they also escaped during 1607-8 to Amsterdam. It is uncertain whether they there united again with their former associates at Gainsborough or not, but there is evidence that they maintained a separate existence as a church. At any rate it is recorded that certain peculiar opinions held by Mr.

Smyth bred trouble in his church, resulting in the exclusion of himself and some of his followers, and that the cautious, peaceable Robinson and his company determined to seek another place of residence.

They therefore transferred themselves to the neighboring city of Leyden, where Robinson spent the remaining sixteen years of his life and won and exerted most of the influence which has made him famous. In January, 1611, he joined three of his friends — William Jepson, Henry Wood, and Randall Thickins — in the purchase of a house and garden on the Klocksteeg, almost opposite St. Peter's, the cathedral church, and only a block or two from the university. They promised to give for this estate eight thousand gilders — as much as twelve thousand dollars or more in our modern money [5] — paying two thousand gilders down and giving a mortgage for the balance with a pledge of an annual payment of five

SITE OF JOHN ROBINSON'S HOUSE IN LEYDEN.
House with arched door.

hundred gilders. Robinson's superior education doubtless stood him in good stead and he appears to have become able in time to live with at least modest comfort.

But it cannot be inferred certainly from his joining the other purchasers of the estate just mentioned that he had accumulated much property. It is much more probable that he was not raised conspicuously above what is known to have been the poverty of most of his associates. He may have become a partner in the purchase merely in his official capacity, the others supplying most or the whole of the funds. Indeed, it is very likely that the whole company subscribed the money, as the purchase seems to have been made for the common benefit, and chose the four whose names appear as a committee to act in behalf of all. They took possession on May 1, 1612, and the estate at once became the headquarters of their company.[6] They soon built twenty-one little houses in the garden so that a considerable number of them were enabled to live together in a sort of colony. Robinson and his family lived in the large house, and they also used it as their place of public worship.

Six years after settling in Leyden, Robinson became a member, as a student of theology,[7] of its famous university, perhaps in some such relation to it as that of the modern post-graduate student. Why he did not join it sooner can only be conjectured. But in 1615 he obtained the necessary permission of the magistrates of the city, was matriculated and at once assumed its peculiar civil[8] as well as intellectual privileges. In the university circles he found congenial company and his worth was recognized speedily. Before very long a sharp theological controversy broke out between the followers of Arminius and the Old Calvinists, and, at the urging of the latter, whose views he held, he engaged several times, and with honor, in public debate with Professor Episcopius.

He had adopted the then unusual course of attending the lectures of the opposite party, in order to understand both sides, so that he was well qualified to argue against it.

With the exception of this incident little is known in detail of his career for several years. We are only aware that he was associated closely and tenderly with his Pilgrim companions; that he was their faithful pastor and also their teacher, the aged Clifton having remained in Amsterdam; that they regarded him as their best friend and wisest adviser; that his church grew until it numbered about three hundred communicants; that he wrote and published several books of a theological or religious character; and that he corresponded with faithful Separatists who had remained in England about the possibilities and prospects of Nonconformity. When the practical question rose whether the Pilgrims ought not to emigrate afresh and to the new world across the Atlantic, he largely shaped their decision and forwarded their departure. It was decided that only a part of the company should go at once, but that the others, the majority, should follow in due time, and that Robinson should remain with those who at first stayed behind. On July 11, 1620, the final decisions were made, and eleven days later, on July 22, the emigrants set sail in the Speedwell from Delfshaven.

Less than five years remained to him and they were saddened by domestic affliction. It is recorded that on February 7, 1621, "a child of the English preacher" was buried in St. Peter's, and probably this was one of his family. He is enrolled in the city census as dwelling, on October 15, 1622, in the Groenport on the Klocksteeg with his wife, Bridget, their children, John, Bridget, Isaac, Mercy, Fear, and James, and their servant, Mary Hardy. Another and similar burial record, dated March 27, 1623, indicates that a second child of his then was interred in St.

Peter's. Upon March 4, 1625, he too was buried somewhere therein, the pastors of the various city churches and also representatives of the university attending his funeral. The sum paid for his burial, nine florins, the largest sum then customarily paid unless exceptional privileges were granted, shows that probably he was in at least comfortable circumstances when he died.

He was a profoundly spiritual Christian in an age when spirituality was rare. He also was eminently genial and lovable. He was a thorough, accurate scholar. Bradford says of him: "He was never satisfied in himself until he had searched every cause or argument he had to deal in to the bottom."[9] He was cautious and far-sighted in judgment and energetic in action. In Brewster, Bradford, and others he had able coadjutors, but he was their acknowledged leader. Moreover, his scholarship, his conscientious Calvinism, and his forensic powers rendered him a champion in the broader field of the public discussions of the time. He also was an independent thinker, and, as we shall presently see, he taught and practiced a Congregationalism almost as pure as that of the apostolic churches. Yet in an age conspicuous for bigotry he was a noble example of tolerance. He insisted that there were many true Christians in the English Church and that Separatists sometimes would do well to attend its worship.

There are two opinions of his meaning in his famous saying that "the Lord God had more truth and light yet to breake forth out of his Holy Word," but careful study of its connection and circumstances establishes the probability that it had reference to ecclesiastical polity rather than to general spiritual enlightenment.[10] In either case it shows him to have been far in advance of his age. He was one of the comparatively few men in human history whose character and work seem

ROBINSON MEMORIAL TABLET.

nobler the more they are studied, and whose renown is certain to go on increasing hereafter. His publications were eight in number, all of which exist in modern reprints. They are these: *The Answer to a Censorious Epistle* (1608 or 1609); *A Justification of Separation from the Church of England* (1610); *Of Religious Communion, Public and Private* (1614); *A Treatise of the Lawfulness of Hearing of the Ministers in the Church of England* (1634) [*written* 1623-25]; *A Defense of the Doctrine Propounded by the Synode at Dort* (1624); *The People's Plea for the Exercise of Prophesie; Just and Necessarie Apologie* (1625); *Observations Divine and Morall* (1625).

It should be added that, in 1865, Professor George E. Day, D.D., and the late Dr. Henry M. Dexter caused to be inserted in the wall of the house upon the site of Robinson's home in Leyden a stone inscribed, "On this spot lived, taught, and died John Robinson, 1611-1625"; and that on July 24, 1891, a large bronze tablet in his honor, affixed to the outside of St. Peter's church, nearly opposite to his house, was dedicated, having been erected by the National Council of the Congregational Churches of the United States.[11]

CHAPTER VIII.

OTHER SCROOBY PILGRIMS AND THE DECISION TO EMIGRATE.

ALLUSIONS exist to a few others who probably were members of the Scrooby company, and in the lamentable absence of full information they deserve mention. Hunter states that Robert Rochester and Richard Jackson,[1] from Scrooby, belonged to the Gainsborough church and probably they helped to form that at Scrooby. At any rate, they were condemned with Brewster in August, 1608, by the Commissioners of Causes Ecclesiastical for not obeying a summons to appear at the Collegiate Church, Southwell, and the three were fined £20 apiece.[2] Elizabeth Neal is likely to have been another, for the Leyden records — which declare her betrothal[3] to William Buckram on November 30, 1611, and their marriage on December 17 of the same year — also note that she was from Scrooby. Edward Southworth,[4] who, according to Hunter, was from Basset Lawe, the "hundred," or civil district, which included Scrooby, apparently was a Pilgrim who accompanied the others to Leyden and died there, his widow Alice (Carpenter) later, at Plymouth, Mass., becoming the second wife of William Bradford.

Francis Jessop also, whose estate was in Tilne, and who was of "a wealthy and considerable family," probably was one of the Scrooby church. He had been married to Frances White in Worksop[5] near by on January 24, 1605, and was admitted to citizenship in Leyden on May 5, 1625. But neither he nor any other of those just mentioned, except Mrs. Southworth, came to America. Doubtless many others who were members of the Pilgrim body in Leyden had come from Scrooby or its vicinity, for it was a considerable company

Other Scrooby Pilgrims.

which fled from England. Bradford says that "a large companie of them purposed to get passage at Boston"[6] and it is recorded that the number of those who subsequently received permission to settle in Leyden, which evidently included most, if not nearly the whole, of the company from Scrooby, was "one hundred persons or thereabouts."[7] But it is now impossible to determine who the others were, excepting perhaps George Morton, and the evidence in his case is not complete.

A short distance northwest of Bawtry there had lived for some generations, at the least, a family named Morton. Hunter quotes Sir Egerton Brydges as calling it one of "the historical families" of England. It had a fine estate, which now has dwindled to a large farm, but which still is so valuable that it changed hands in 1891 for $150,000. Back in Roman Catholic times one of this family endowed a little chapel and an almshouse for a few poor old women, which still stand close by the entrance to the grounds of Bawtry Hall, yet actually in the next parish, and, although no longer in the hands of Roman Catholics, continue their useful services. The Leyden records state that on August 2, 1612, one George Morton, a merchant, who had come from York in England, was married to Juliana Carpenter. There is no absolute proof, but it probably is true that he was one of this family of Mortons and had grown up in the neighborhood of the Pilgrims in England, and that, after passing at York some time subsequent to their departure, he followed them to Leyden. There were other and humbler Mortons in or near Austerfield, and he may have been one of them, but he is known to have been a man of so much education and leadership that he is much more likely to have come of the superior stock. Moreover, just at this time one of its representatives certainly bore his name, and Hunter speaks of this one as "unaccounted for,"[8] which implies a large possibility of his identity with his Pilgrim namesake. At any rate, Morton became prominent among them in Holland and went to England several times in their interest. He aided in completing the arrangements for their voyage to America, and intended to accompany them in the Mayflower, but he remained for a time in England, where he wrote the introduction to and superintended the publication of the work describing their early American experiences, which, from his connection with it, came to be called *Mourt's Relation*. He finally followed them with his immediate family to Plymouth in 1623 in the Anne and died in less than a year thereafter, much respected and mourned.[9] These few facts seem to be all hitherto ascertained about the Scrooby Pilgrims personally.

It is difficult to form a completely trustworthy estimate of their means, their social position, and the degrees of their culture from such meager data as we possess. It is not probable that any member of the company, as it existed at Scrooby, was of noble ancestry, unless this may have been true of George Morton. But Clifton,[10] Brewster, and Jessop, at the least, appear to have belonged to the gentry of the region. Evidently the company included representatives of different ranks in society. Their subsequent poverty and the humble character of the occupations in which most of them engaged after reaching Holland are easily explained by the facts that in exiling themselves they must have been obliged, as the rule, to sell what property they had in England — so far as this could be done at all — at a heavy sacrifice and probably by stealth, and were forced to support themselves by any labor open to strangers ignorant of the Dutch tongue and more familiar with the care of land than with manufacturing or trading. Probably most of them were fairly well educated for the times and moderately well off pecuniarily, and none but persons of sterling character would have engaged in their undertaking.

The story of their flight from their English homes now must be told. As has been suggested, their young church for a short time probably escaped the hostility of the authorities. But their tranquillity did not endure long. The severities with which other Separatists were treated soon began to be visited upon them. The state of things became so evil that Bradford says : —

> They could not long continue in any peaceable condition, but were hunted & persecuted on every side, so as their former afflictions were but as fleabitings in comparison of these which now came upon them. For some were taken & clapt up in prison, others had their houses besett & watcht night and day, & hardly escaped their hands ; and ye most were faine to flie & leave their howses & habitations, and the meanes of their livelehood.[11]

This was intolerable. Evidently it was only the renewal of previous persecutions of which no specific record remains. There could be but one outcome, and Bradford adds : —

> Seeing them selves thus molested, and that ther was no hope of ther continuance ther, by a joynte consente they resolved to goe into yᵉ Low-Countries, wher they heard was freedom of Religion for all men; as also how sundrie from London, & other parts of yᵉ land, had been exiled and persecuted for yᵉ same cause, & were gone thither, and lived at Amsterdam, & in other places of yᵉ land. So affter they had continued togeither aboute a year, and kept their meetings every Saboth in one place or other, exercising the worship of God amongst them selves, notwithstanding all yᵉ dilligence & malice of their adverssaries, they seeing they could no longer continue in yᵗ condition, they resolved to get over into Hollād as they could.[12]

This would have been a serious undertaking indeed, even if they had been permitted to depart freely. Most of them must have known Holland only by report. There is no evidence that any one of them, except Brewster, ever had been in or near to that country or anywhere else out of

England. Its language and customs were strange. It was a costly country in which to live, and how they were to support themselves they did not know. Few among them can have been other than farmers, and they must have been largely unfamiliar with the Dutch methods in agriculture, and, as they specially desired to keep together as a body, it was important for them to make their new homes in some city or town and not to distribute themselves at random wherever employment might be obtainable most readily. Moreover, Holland was peculiarly exposed to the miseries of war, being the object of frequent invasions by the Spaniards. It is easy to imagine how much weight these objections must have had, how long and anxiously they must have reflected and compared convictions as to their duty, and how reluctantly they must have decided at last that they ought to depart.

The providence of God seemed to leave them no other practicable alternative. In

Holland, whatever its disadvantages and even perils might prove to be, they were sure of attaining the one privilege for the sake of which they were willing to surrender every other — freedom to worship God in what they believed to be his own ordained way. Bradford says upon this point : —

> These things did not dismay them (though they did some times trouble them) for their desires were sett on ye ways of God, & to injoye his ordinances ; but they rested on his providence, & knew whom they had beleeved.[13]

They had no pillar of cloud by day and of fire by night to assure them that the Almighty was watching over and guiding them, but they went forth at last with a reverent faith in him, which, perhaps, was as firm as a direct command from above could have rendered it.

CHAPTER IX.

THE EMIGRATION TO HOLLAND.

AS has been explained, no practicable alternative remained to the Scrooby church but to depart from England. As Bradford puts it, they were "constrained to leave their native soyle and countrie, their lands & livings, and all their freinds & famillier acquaintance." Yet, although they could not stay, they were not allowed to emigrate freely. The legal and ecclesiastical authorities interposed every possible hindrance, not hesitating to employ trickery and even actual force. No description can be more suggestive than the pathetic language which Bradford used years afterwards when narrating their experience : —

> Though they could not stay, yet were ye not suffered to goe, but ye ports & havens were shut

against them, soe as they were faine to seeke secrete means of conveance, & to bribe & fee ye mariners, & give exterordinarie rates for their passages. And yet were they often times betrayed (many of them), and both they & their goods intercepted & surprised, and therby put to great trouble & charge.[1]

For example, in 1607 a large number of them hired a ship, intending to sail from some place agreed upon but now unknown near Boston on the Lincolnshire coast. Of course it would not have been safe to embark in the town. The master settled with them upon the day and the place of embarkation. But he failed to keep the appointment and a long delay ensued, which caused them heavy expense and of course serious anxiety. At last he did appear in the nighttime and took them and their goods aboard, but only to betray them. He had connived with the authorities for their capture. The officers promptly arrested them. They were put into open boats and taken ashore, their persons, even those of the women, being searched with gross indignities. Stripped of money, books, and much other property, they were carried back into the town through inquisitive crowds, taken before the magistrates, and then imprisoned.

It is pleasant to be told that the magistrates "used them courteously, and shewed them what favour they could," although having no power to release them. The case had to be laid before the lords of the council, so settled was the policy of the government not to allow even peaceable and otherwise inoffensive persons to disregard the statutes requiring conformity, and, there being then neither telegraphs nor the modern postal service, messengers had to be employed, no matter how long the accused remained in prison awaiting trial. They were kept in jail for a whole month and then, although their lordships of the council dismissed the greater part of them, seven of the leaders were continued in prison and bound over for further trial at the next assizes. Who these seven were is not stated, but Brewster was one,[2] and there can be little doubt that Robinson and Bradford also were among them. It is stated that those set at liberty were "sent to ye places from whence they came." Probably they had no other alternative but to return sadly to Scrooby, or wherever else they had lived, and try to resume their former life as best they could, while waiting to see what new hope the future might afford.

They were not daunted, however, and in the spring of the next year, 1608, they made another attempt. Their seven leaders appear to have been again free. Apparently distrusting their own countrymen, they this time engaged at Hull a Dutch captain from Zeland. They told him their pitiable history frankly, "hoping to find more faithfullnes in him, then in ye former of their owne nation," and he promised to be loyal to them. Between Grimsby and Hull, on the bay formed by the mouth of the Humber, they knew of a lonely stretch of shore, "a large comone a good way distante from any towne." There this captain agreed to meet and embark them. Thither, therefore, they sent the women and children the previous day in a small vessel, the men planning to follow by land. The little vessel with its precious load reached the rendezvous, but the roughness of the sea had made the passengers ill, so that the vessel was run for shelter into a small creek, where she grounded at low tide. The next morning the Dutch captain appeared, as agreed, but the transfer of passengers could not be made until high tide, about noon.

Meanwhile the men of the company came. The shipmaster sent his boats to embark them, but as soon as the first boat-load had been shipped the work had to be abandoned. There appeared "a greate company, both horse & foote, with bills & gunes, & other weapons; for ye countrie was raised to take them." Whether the emigrants had been watched constantly by spies, or their renewed disappearance from home had been detected at once, or their progress through the country to the coast, which must have been slow and impossible to be wholly concealed, had attracted notice, is matter of conjecture. It is remarkable, not that they were discovered and pursued, but that they so nearly escaped. The Dutchman "swore his countries oath 'sacremente,'" and having a fair wind made sail at once, and was not to blame for so doing, inasmuch as his remaining could not have benefited the emigrants and doubtless would have involved him personally in serious consequences — probably his own imprisonment and the loss of his ship.

The plight of the Pilgrims was pitiable indeed. The few men who had succeeded in embarking, of whom Bradford evidently was one, were compelled to leave their families and companions visibly doomed to arrest and renewed persecution. Moreover, most of their money and clothing for the voyage, together with what other little property they had, was on the smaller vessel with the women and children. They sailed away, not only in distress and fear for those left behind, but also in great bodily discomfort, "not having a cloath to shifte them with, more then they had on their baks, & some scarce a peney aboute them, all they had being abord ye barke." To make matters worse they at once encountered a heavy gale. For seven days "they neither saw son, moone, nor stars." They were driven almost to the coast of Norway and barely escaped foundering, the ship actually once being given up for lost by her crew, who abandoned themselves to despair and disorder, and her escape seeming to them, by the record, hardly less than a miracle. The voyage, which was expected to occupy not over two or three days, lasted for two whole weeks, but at last they reached their destined port in safety. The length and severity of the storm had been phenomenal. It had done great damage generally and their arrival in port caused much popular astonishment at their survival.

As for those left behind, all the men, except as many as were believed necessary to assist the women and children, prudently scattered and escaped. The others of the company were arrested at once in a condition of mind and body easier to be imagined than borne. The artless record is significant : —

> But pitifull it was to see ye heavie case of these poore women in this distress; what weeping & crying on every side, some for their husbands, that were caried away in ye ship as is before related; others not knowing what should become of them, & their litle ones; others againe melted in teares, seeing their poore litle ones aboute them, crying for feare, and quaking with could.

They proved a burden to their captors after all. Says Bradford : —

> They were hurried from one place to another, and from one justice to another, till in ye ende they

The Emigration to Holland. 115

knew not what to doe with them; for to imprison so many women & innocent children for no other cause (many of them) but that they must goe with their husbands, semed to be unreasonable and all would crie out of them; and to send them home againe was as difficult, for they aledged, as ye trueth was, they had no homes to goe to, for they had either sould, or otherwise disposed of their houses & livings. To be shorte, after they had been thus turmoyled a good while, and conveyed from one constable to another, they were glad to be ridd of them in ye end upon any termes; for all were wearied & tired with them. Though in ye mean time they (poore soules) indured miserie enough; and thus in ye end necessitie forste a way for them.

There may have been some popular sympathy with them in the Lincolnshire region. Certainly some of the local authorities were disinclined to treat them with extreme severity. Possibly the harshness shown them had overreached itself and had awakened compassion for them. Probably it was due chiefly to orders and superior officials sent from London, whom the people of the region did not dare to oppose, yet did not heartily approve. In any case, however, the sufferings of the Pilgrims were grievous. Yet the hand of God was in that which befell them, overruling it for good. A fitting close of the story is found in these further words of Bradford: —

Yet I may not omitte ye fruite that came hearby, for by these so publick troubls, in so many eminente places, their cause became famouss, & occasioned many to looke into ye same; and their godly cariage & Christian behaviour was such as left a deep impression in the minds of many. And though some few shrunk at these first conflicts & sharp beginings (as it was no marvel,) yet many more came on with fresh courage, & greatly animated others.

It must be remembered that these are oniy two of the bitter experiences which the Pilgrims underwent in their endeavor to escape from England. But, as Bradford adds: —

In ye end, notwithstanding all these stormes of oppossition, they all gatt over at length, some at one time & some at an other, and some in one place & some in an other, and mette togeather againe according to their desires, with no small rejoycing.

Robinson, Brewster, and other principal members, it is recorded, were among the last to go, having stayed to help the weaker ones off before departing themselves.

CHAPTER X.

IN AMSTERDAM.

UPON reaching Holland the Pilgrims naturally made Amsterdam their home at first, partly, probably, because in so large a city they seemed likely to find occupation most readily and partly because they already had friends there who also sympathized with their religious convictions. There were English Congregationalists there before them. Our story primarily is that of the Pilgrims, but at this point, in order to understand the situation as they found it, it is necessary to consider briefly some facts in the history of these other Congregationalists who had preceded them thither.

Before his martyrdom John Penry advised his London associates to emigrate.[1] Afterwards the English government perceived that it had gone too far and that a wiser policy would permit the Separatists to leave the country. Indeed, it apparently released some from jail upon condition of emigration.[2] This spasm of official good sense did not last long, but some advantage was taken of it. In the year of Penry's death, 1593, a few of the London Brownists fled to Holland and soon established themselves in Amsterdam.[3] Others followed, and by the end of 1595 there were several hundreds. They were so poor as to be aided by the city and by friends in England. They maintained their worship; and apparently their pastor, Francis Johnson, with their elders, joined them in 1597, Henry Ainsworth previously having become their teacher.

Johnson,[4] born about 1562, probably at Richmond, in Yorkshire, and his brother George, two years younger, were Cambridge graduates and he was a Fellow of Christ's College. In 1588 he declared himself a Presbyterian and was imprisoned. He soon recanted, but not satisfactorily. He was expelled from the university in 1589, evidently because of his beliefs, was again imprisoned, and upon release went to Middleburgh in Zeland and became pastor of a church of English merchants. In 1591 a book by Barrowe and Greenwood, the *Plaine Refvtation of M. Giffard's Booke, etc.*, — after he had complained of it in behalf of the English ambassador and had caused all but two copies to be burned, — converted him to its views. Resigning, he went to London, visited Barrowe in the Fleet Prison, and joined the new Congregational church in 1592, becoming its pastor. On December 5, he too was imprisoned. During his imprisonment a little treatise, *A True Confession of the Faith, etc.*, was published, the authorship of which he shared. His brother George was his fellow believer and also was shut up for preaching. After part of the church had gone to Holland troubles arose among those left in London.

Francis Johnson, while in prison, married a widow whose manner of dress gave offense and caused differences between the brothers themselves and disturbed some of their followers. In 1597 the Johnsons were released that they might emigrate to Rainea, one of the Magdalen Islands in the Gulf of St. Lawrence. But the expedition failed, and in September, with most of their companions, they were in Amsterdam with their predecessors.

The church — although apparently a portion of its membership still remained in London — thus became complete in organization again, its officers being Francis Johnson, pastor; Henry Ainsworth, teacher; Daniel Studley, George Knyveton, and M. Slade, elders; and Christopher Bowman, deacon.[5] The disagreement about Mrs. Johnson's apparel revived. George Johnson opposed his brother, several angry church meetings were held, and the issue became involved with ecclesiastical questions. The father of the Johnsons went to Amsterdam hoping to reconcile them, but at last both he and his son George were excommunicated. Meanwhile Francis Johnson had published two treatises, one original, the other a reissue of that by Barrowe and Greenwood which he formerly had caused to be burned. Some discussion about church principles also had been held with Dutch theologians and a deputation and a petition had been sent vainly to King James after his accession for leave to return to England. Moreover, one Thomas White with a few companions from the west of England also had joined them for a time, later forming a church of their own.[6]

At about this point, in 1606, the Gainsborough emigrants, headed by John Smyth, appeared in Amsterdam.[7] Smyth also was a Cambridge graduate, of Christ's College, in 1575-76, and became a Fellow in 1579.[8] Ten years later he advocated so strict a Sabbath-keeping that he was cited before the university authorities. Later he was preacher to the city of Lincoln. He studied the question of leaving the State Church nine months and held a public disputation about it before withdrawing. In 1602 he gathered the Congregational church in Gainsborough, which has been mentioned already, and in 1606 the majority of this body under his lead went over to Amsterdam. Here they probably did not unite with Johnson's church but maintained an independent though at first not unfriendly existence.[9] Smyth was an able scholar and preacher, and he had some medical knowledge and was very kind to the poor, but he often was injudicious and must have been an extremist in his opinions and dogmatic and sometimes intolerant in urging them. He soon began to advocate a somewhat new form of Congregationalism and published several treatises criticizing Johnson's church for its errors. Several of his charges were trivial, but one point, that the Scriptures declare the offices of pastor, teacher, and elder to be not three and different but one and the same, was an important step toward the modern theory.[10]

Thus there appear to have been two Congregational churches in Amsterdam by 1608, having Francis Johnson and Smyth for their respective pastors. A third, of which White perhaps was pastor, also may still have been in existence, although its life evidently was brief. The two other churches formed by the expulsion of Smyth and the secession of Ainsworth had not then come into being. This sketch of the fortunes of the London and Gainsborough churches shows that there were foolish men as well as wise among the earlier emigrants, and that some who ought to have been among the wisest occasionally rivaled the folly of the most foolish. Too much heed was given to trifles, and in vital matters there was too little of a conciliatory and fraternal temper. Most of them were very poor and socially they must have been obscure.

They had managed to exist, but hardly can be said to have prospered. Yet they had secured religious freedom and had practiced Congregationalism as they understood it. It is gratifying to know, also, that, after the absurd disputes about Mrs. Johnson's clothes had been settled and after Smyth and his followers had seceded, Francis Johnson's church enjoyed a short period of real prosperity. Bradford, forty years later, wrote: —

If you had seen them in their beauty and order, as we have done, you would have been much affected therewith, we dare say. At Amsterdam, before their division and breach [apparently subsequent to what has been mentioned], they were about three hundred communicants.[11]

But all too soon new trouble arose, this time in Smyth's church. He conceived that valid baptism involves the intelligent assent of the subject of the rite. So he reorganized his church, limiting its membership to consenting adults. He did not insist upon immersion, however, but practiced affusion, and, nobody being obtainable to administer the rite who, on his theory, had been properly baptized, he rebaptized first himself and then his associate pastor, Helwys, and the others.[12] We need not follow their fortunes. Bradford sums up the case by saying that they "(for ye most part) buried them selves & their names."

To the Pilgrim body the existing condition naturally was uninviting. There is some doubt whether they united themselves with Johnson's company, but it is probable that they kept themselves apart as a church.[13] They remained in Amsterdam about a year, but in six months, perceiving that to stay there must involve them in the disagreements of their predecessors,[14] from which their peace-loving disposition repelled them, they determined to make another remove. They asked and received official permission to settle in Leyden,[15] and by midsummer the transfer was made. Apparently not above six months more passed before Johnson's church was rent again by grave differences and the outcome was the secession of Ainsworth and others, who formed a church of their own almost next door to that abandoned.[16]

Ainsworth [17] personally was a learned, godly man, one of the best of the early Congregationalists. He was a native of Swanton Morley, Norfolk, England, in 1570, studied at St. John's College and later at Gonville and Caius College, Cambridge, perhaps spent some time in Ireland, and was in Amsterdam in 1593, probably as a bookseller's porter. He was an expert linguist.[18] In 1596 he became the teacher in Johnson s church. He was, probably with Johnson, the author of the *True Confession of Faith of the People Called Brownists*, and he wrote not less than twenty-eight other publications.[19] In 1610, as the outcome of a difference between himself and Johnson, Ainsworth claiming that the power of excommunication rests with the whole church and Johnson that it belongs to the church officers only, he and others withdrew. The Leyden church was called upon for advice, but its suggestions seem to have been disregarded. Johnson and his adherents excommunicated Ainsworth and his followers, and a lawsuit for the possession of the church building occupied by the former ensued, which appears to have been won by the latter. Smyth having died in 1612, his later followers joined a Dutch church, and the other members of his original church having returned to England, and White's little company also having disappeared, Ainsworth's church thus finally became the sole representative of Separatism in the city, at any rate for a time, Johnson also with his friends removing elsewhere.[20]

The history of these Amsterdam Congregationalists is sad and even shameful, but it throws into the more bold relief the harmony and wisdom which the Scrooby

Pilgrims illustrated. From all such scandals their record was wholly free. It is worth noting here that the visitor to modern Amsterdam may see in a narrow lane called *Bruingang* (Brown Alley), leading from the *Barndesteeg*, a venerable building upon the site where one of the Brownist congregations worshiped. Which church this was is not now known, but the history of the spot identifies it with one of them. Robinson and his associates may not have worshiped there, but the spot must have been familiar to them.

CHAPTER XI.

IN LEYDEN.

WHEN the Pilgrims were planning to abandon Amsterdam as a residence, Leyden, which then contained nearly or quite 100,000 people, was, in the words of Bradford, "a fair & bewtifull citie, and of a sweet situation, but made more famous by ye universitie wherwith it is adorned, in which of late had been so many learned men." Their first step was to obtain leave to settle there and the Leyden records state that "John Robinson"—*Jan Robartse* the Dutch wrote his name—"minister of the Divine Word, and some of the members of the Christian Reformed Religion born in the kingdom of Great Britain, to the number of one hundred persons, or thereabouts, men and women," petitioned the Leyden magistrates for permission to remove to that city "by the 1st May next and to have the freedom thereof in carrying on their trades without being a burden in the least to any one." This is undated, but the official response was recorded on February 12, 1609, and runs thus:—

> The Court, in making a disposition of this present memorial, declare that they refuse no honest persons free ingress to come and have their residence in this city, provided that such persons behave themselves, and submit to the laws and ordinances; and therefore the coming of the memorialists will be agreeable and welcome.[1]

By midsummer they had availed themselves of this permission.

It is not known in what part of the city they settled at first, but it has been conjectured that they probably found homes upon what was then its newer border, near its northwest limit, in St. Ursula Street and the vicinity. But the city, "wanting that traffike by sea which Amsterdam enjoys, it was not so beneficiall for their outward means of living & estats." They did not lose heart, however. "Being now hear pitchet they fell to such trads & imployments as they best could." As has been said, Brewster taught English and later set up a printing press.[2] Edward Winslow, who first joined them here, also was a printer. George Morton, Samuel Butter, John Jennings, and Edward Pickering became merchants, doubtless in a small way. Most of the others were compelled to and, indeed, in view of their different training were only fit for humbler labors, and they were employed variously. Edmund Jessop and Henry Collins made bombazine. William Bradford, Samuel Fuller, Edward Southworth, and Roger Wilson were fustian workers, fustian being a kind of serge. Cuthbert Cuthbertson and Samuel Lee made hats. Robert Cushman and Richard Masterson combed or carded wool, and William Bassett supported himself as a hod carrier. Others were weavers of baize, carpenters, masons, twine spinners, makers of pipes, gloves, candles, blocks, clocks, pumps, or cabinets, or stocking weavers, bakers, brewers, coopers, or tailors.[3] "At length they came to raise a competente & comforteable living, but with hard and continuall labor."

Thus they went on for eleven years, "injoying much sweete & delightefull societie & spirituall comforte togeather in ye wayes of God." It is not known where they worshiped during the first two years, but after they had received possession of the estate on the Klocksteeg already described,[4] on May 1, 1612, they appear to have held their services there.[5] Here they were joined by others from England, "so as they grew a great congregation," numbering at last nearly or quite three hundred. Their history as a church is not recorded in detail. They "lived togeather in peace, & love, and holines." That occasional friction, due to natural human imperfection, occurred is implied in Bradford's language:—

If at any time any differences arose, or offences broak out (as it cannot be, but some time ther will, even amongst yᵉ best of men) they were ever so mete with, & nipt in yᵉ head betims, or otherwise so well composed, as still love, peace, and communion was continued; or els yᵉ church purged of those that were incurable & incorrigible, when after much patience used, no other means would serve, which seldom came to pass.⁶

But these words also show how rarely and how little their spiritual peace and growth were thus disturbed.

Furthermore, they never lost their good outward repute. Bradford declares in reply to certain " slanders against them," uttered evidently by English enemies, that

First though many of them weer poore, yet ther was none so poore, but if they were known to be of yᵗ congregation, the *Dutch* (either bakers or others) would trust them in any reasonable matter when yᵉʸ wanted money. Because they had found by experience how carfull they were to keep their word, and saw them so painfull & dilligente in their callings; yea, they would strive to gett their custome, and to imploy them above others, in their worke, for their honestie & dilligence.

Againe; ye magistrats of ye citie, aboute ye time of their coming away, or a litle before, in ye publick place of justice, gave this comendable testemoney of them, in ye reproofe of the Wallons, who were of ye French church in y^t citie. These English, said they, have lived amongst us now this 12. years, and yet we never had any sute or accusation came against any of them; but your strifs & quarrels are continuall.[7]

During these laborious and severe yet comparatively tranquil years, they enjoyed the religious freedom which they had fled from England to obtain. Most of them, however, remained poor and obscure. William Bradford, Isaac Allerton, Digory Priest, Thomas Rogers, Thomas Tinker, and John Turner, who came in the Mayflower, and Edmund Chandler, Henry Colet, Christopher Ellis, Abraham Grey, William Jepson, and John Keble, who remained in Leyden, were admitted to citizenship before the emigration, and Francis Jessop, Stephen Butterfield, and

Henry Jepson afterwards.[8] It may have been true of Robinson, for on September 5, 1615, he was matriculated as a member of the university, which secured him some special civil privileges. Thomas Brewer had been similarly admitted to the university on February 17 of the same year, and John Greenwood also was matriculated in 1625. But matriculation may not have involved actual citizenship then any more than it now does at Yale or Harvard.

Almost the sole evidence of the emergence of any one of the company into publicity is the invitation, pressed upon Robinson and at last accepted by him, from Professor Poliander to defend Calvinism in public debate with Professor Episcopius. Public feeling in theological circles, which were relatively wider than they are now, ran very high just at this time upon the subject, and political considerations seem to have been more or less involved. This task Robinson performed with evident reluctance. "He was loath, being a stranger," — clearly he had not become widely known in the city, — but yielded, being told "that ye truth would suffer if he did not help them." When the day came, says Bradford, whose testimony, although naturally disposed to be favorable, there is no reason to dispute and which Edward Winslow indorsed,[9]

> The Lord did so help him to defend ye truth & foyle this adversarie, as he put him to an apparent nonplus, in this great & publike audience. And ye like he did a 2. or 3. time, upon such like occasions. The which as it caused many to praise God y^t the trueth had so famous victory, so it procured him much honour & respecte from those lerned men & others which loved ye trueth.[10]

But there is no evidence that Bradford or Brewster or any others who later became prominent in America were in any way conspicuous in Leyden except in their own body. The welcome and the treatment which the Pilgrims received in Holland, and the impression made by them, can be understood best by imagining a parallel case to-day. Suppose a company of Hollanders, for instance, mostly of little more than local importance at home, but intelligent, industrious, religious, and desirous of greater liberty in belief and worship, to petition the authorities of an American city for leave to settle therein. They would receive a favorable reply similar in formality and courtesy to that given the Pilgrims. Suppose them, upon arrival, to find what employment they could, to win a good name among their neighbors and employers for integrity and diligence and, in the course of a dozen years, with the civil authorities for their orderliness. Suppose twelve or fourteen of them to become voters in due time, and two or three of the best educated to join the local university, one of these, the pastor of the body, proving an able debater and finally gaining a good reputation in public discussion, most of his companions still and always remaining plain, humble, and useful but obscure working people.

This imaginary case would be a precise reproduction of that of the Pilgrims in Holland. It is probably a mistake to suppose that as a body they ever attracted much attention in Leyden. The perils of the times, which led public authorities to keep well informed concerning all classes of the population, doubtless caused the Pilgrims and their doings to be known to the magistrates officially, and their immediate neighbors, their employers, and others of course had more or less to do with them; but probably much the larger part of the population, including most of the leaders in business and society, knew little or nothing of their presence.

The Leyden of to-day, quite as truly as the modern Scrooby and its vicinity, looks substantially as it did in the time of the Pilgrims. The Old and the New Rhines flow through it in their ancient channels and with the same lazy currents and are thronged with craft of the same clumsy shapes, and the numerous canals which intersect it and have given it its familiar title, "the Venice of the North," and the one hundred and fifty bridges which cross them, are the same as then. So, too, is the Burg, the low hill at the junction of the two Rhines, thrown up by human hands centuries ago to support the little castle which once crowned its summit, the only such mound within miles. The cathedral church, St. Peter's, and its almost equally stately companion, St. Pancras and St. Mary's, as well as the quaint and dignified city hall and the university, are essentially unaltered in appearance. Moreover, the general impression made by the architecture of the ordinary houses, and the low, flat, fertile country which surrounds the city, must be just what it was when they were there. A row of little dwellings which used to nestle against the wall of St. Peter's, opposite to their estate on the Klocksteeg, has been torn down, and other houses elsewhere have been removed or rebuilt, and there are larger windows in the shops and occasional horse-cars in a few of the streets. But many of the women still wear the picturesque provincial costumes formerly worn, and no violent effort of the imagination is demanded in order to revive the look of things as the Pilgrims saw them. No student of the past can fail to be grateful that all this is true.

CHAPTER XII.

THE DEVELOPMENT OF CONGREGATIONALISM.

IT is now well to pause in the study of the personal history of the Pilgrims long enough to observe the gradual development of Congregationalism up to their departure from Holland to America. Several successive phases have been noted which deserve to be explained and compared a little more definitely.

The first was Brownism.[1] Robert Browne taught not only separation from the State Church but also the absolute independence of each local church, as well as the fellowship of these severally independent churches. Church authority, he held, rests purely in the lordship of Christ over each such local body of believers. Its individual members are to interpret,

Plymouth Rock and Canopy.

exercise, and submit to the laws which he has declared. Christ is absolute monarch over his churches, the individual members of which are his vicegerents. This system is practically an absolute monarchy, but Christ is its only sovereign and on earth it is indistinguishable in its results from a pure democracy. It includes among officers of a church not only a pastor, a teacher, deacons, relievers, and widows, but also elders, and it was in connection with the eldership that new developments occurred.

The second phase was Barrowism. Henry Barrowe accepted Browne's principle of the independency of the local church. But he tried to combine with it — apparently distrusting the competence of ordinary church members to manage religious matters, even under the guidance of the Holy Spirit — the theory of the eldership which Thomas Cartwright, the Presbyterian, had advocated. The result was to create Congregational churches governed by Presbyterian boards of elders, an anomalous and illogical combination. As the incongruity between these principles became evident in practice, two forms of Barrowism grew up.

One, the third phase, may be called Johnsonism, because Francis Johnson was its prominent exponent. It also has been termed High-Church Barrowism. Accepting the independence of each local church, it nevertheless insisted upon the right of the body of elders to rule in the church. It withdrew from the other members, after they had elected their elders, all rights except to submit obediently to the decrees of the elders, and, when once elders had been chosen, it gave to them superior power in naming those who should be added to their own number. It was not true Congregationalism.

The other form, the fourth phase, may be termed Ainsworthism, because Henry Ainsworth urged it. It also has been called Low-Church Barrowism. It differed from Johnsonism in that it required the elders to act in harmony with, and recognizing the coequal rights of, the other church members, and not as a superior and ruling body. It held the decisions of the elders to be valid only after indorsement by the other members of a church. This was more like, but even this was not, actual Congregationalism.

The fifth phase was that taught and practiced by John Robinson and the Pilgrim church. It may be called Robinsonism or Broad-Church Barrowism. It was an advance upon Ainsworth's teachings in respect to the eldership. The Leyden church seems never to have had more than one elder,[2] William Brewster, and after he had gone to America it apparently never filled the eldership thus left vacant. Although the office was not abolished formally, it practically ceased to exist in that church. Moreover, the theory of the church — the same theory which the Pilgrims acted upon after reaching America

— was that the elders are neither the church nor the rulers of the church, but merely its moral advisers and leaders. It differed from Ainsworthism less in form than in substance, but the difference, which lay in the fact that it reduced the distinction between elders and their fellow church members to the lowest possible terms, was of the utmost practical significance.

Robinsonism also was an advance upon even Ainsworthism in that it recognized more distinctly the genuineness of churches otherwise organized and in a guarded way permitted and justified communion with them. In his early life, and even while he held the Church of England to be no longer a true church, Robinson gladly conceded that it included many true Christians and that conscientious Separatists properly might unite with them in private, unofficial worship. Later he granted the propriety of "hearing the godly Ministers preach and pray in the publick Assemblies " of that church, and he also favored communion and exchange of members with the Church of Scotland and with the Reformed churches of France and Holland. Moreover, in his *Treatise of the Lawfulnes of Hearing of the Ministers of the Church of England,* he declared that, although he could "not communicate with or submit unto the said church order": —

For myself, thus I believe with my heart before God, and profess with my tongue, and have before the world, that I have one and the same faith, hope, spirit, baptism, and Lord, which I had in the Church of England, and none other; that I esteem so many in that church of what state, or order soever, as are truly partakers of that faith, as I account many thousands to be, for my Christian brethren, and myself a fellow-member with them of that one mystical body of Christ scattered far and wide throughout the world; that I have always, in spirit and affection, all Christian fellowship and communion with them, and am most ready in all outward actions, and exercises of religion, lawful and lawfully done, to express the same: and withal, that I am persuaded, the hearing of the Word of God there preached in the manner, and upon the grounds formerly mentioned, is both lawful and, upon occasion, necessary for me, and all true Christians, withdrawing from that hierarchical order of church government and ministry and appurtenances thereof.[2]

It is needless to consider here such minor episodes as the secession of John Smyth and his followers from fellowship with the Amsterdam Congregationalists under Johnson, which already has been mentioned. Smyth's party certainly took issue with Johnson's partly on grounds of polity, for the former held that it is unscriptural to have a pastor, a teacher, and elders in a church, the pastorate properly including the duties of the two other offices. But this principle, although important in itself, and then a quite new position, does not seem to have been made so prominent in their controversy as others, for example, the alleged sinfulness of using the English text of the Bible instead of the Hebrew and Greek, of using a book in prophesying or in singing, and of allowing non-church members to contribute to the church treasury. Smyth evidently was so eccentric that, probably for this reason, his really valuable contribution to the development of Congregationalism as a polity failed to attract the attention which, if made by a different sort of man, it might have secured.

Such, briefly outlined, was the development of Congregationalism up to the time of the emigration from Holland to America. Its tendency was steadily in the direction of liberty; not a liberty equivalent to license but an intelligent, enlightened, orderly liberty, consistent with and promotive of the highest spiritual development of both the churches, as bodies of believers, and of the individual Christians who composed them. Another step in advance remained to be taken, but the Congregationalism of the Pilgrims was substantially the same with that of modern times. It also deserves to be noted here that during the intervening generations, and recently more than ever, a tendency has been evident in those branches of the Christian Church which have continued to be governed hierarchically toward the restriction of the authority of ecclesiastical officials and toward the increase of the freedom of the body of the laity. Undoubtedly this tendency has been due largely to the influence and example of Congregationalism.

CHAPTER XIII.

THE DEPARTURE FROM HOLLAND.

PROBABLY the Pilgrims cared little about conspicuous prosperity or social eminence in Holland. Could they have secured moderate material comfort and an assured opportunity of desirable moral and spiritual development they would have been content in Leyden. But the opposite was true. The expressions already quoted which testify to their peace and welfare are only to be understood aright when compared with others of a different tenor. That they rejoiced greatly, after their hardships in England, in their new religious liberty is true; and that, because of this liberty, their material condition seemed enjoyable in a real sense, in spite of its severity, also is a fact. But it is not to be inferred that they were situated fortunately as a body even at the best, unless perhaps for a short time. It was their desire to keep chiefly to themselves, to live their own life, and to develop their own ideas of truth. But in the community in which they found themselves this proved impossible.

Most of them continued to be oppressed by poverty and hardship. Bradford declares:—

> Though ye people generally bore all these difficulties very cherfully, & with a resolute courage, being in ye best & strength of their years, yet old age began to steale on many of them, (and their great & continuall labours, with other crosses and sorrows, hastened it before ye time,) so as it was not only probably thought, but apparently seen, that within a few years more they would be in danger to scatter, by necessities pressing them, or sinke under their burdens, or both.[1]

Moreover, their condition was so grievous that it not only rendered them miserable, but also hindered their English sympathizers from joining them in anything like the expected numbers, in which antici-pated union had lain much of their hope for the future. If there were only 10,000 of their fellow Brownists in England by the time of their departure to Holland in 1607–8, and probably there were more,[2] it certainly was not unreason-able in them to suppose that more than two hundred or thereabouts would come over to join them after they had estab-lished themselves.

But no such anticipation was fulfilled.

They saw & found by experience the hardnes of ye place & cuntrie to be such, as few in comparison would come to them, and fewer that would bide it out, and continew with them. For many y^t came to them, and many more y^t desired to be with them, could not endure y^t great labor and hard fare, with other inconveniences which they underwent & were contented with. But though they loved their per-sons, approved their cause, and honored their suf-ferings, yet they left them as it weer weeping. . . . For many, though they desired to injoye ye ordi-nances of God in their puritie, and ye libertie of the gospell with them, yet, alass, they admitted of bondage, with danger of conscience, rather then to indure these hardships; yea, some preferred & chose ye prisons in England, rather then this libertie in Holland, with these afflictions.

The Pilgrims, perhaps, might have endured all these things themselves, but they were wounded in a peculiarly sensitive spot. They were forced to see their children suffer. Bradford remarks pathetically : —

As necessitie was a taskmaster over them, so they were forced to be such, not only to their servants, but in a sorte, to their dearest chilldren; the which as it did not a little wound ye tender harts of many a loving father & mother, so it produced likwise sundrie sad & sorowful effects. For many of their children, that were of best dispositions and gracious inclinations, haveing lernde to bear ye yoake in their youth,· and willing to bear parte of their parents burden, were, often times, so oppressed with their hevie labours, that though their minds were free and willing, yet their bodies bowed under ye weight of ye same, and became decreped in their early youth; the vigor of nature being consumed in ye very budd as it were.

This was bad enough, but it was not the

worst. A danger in their eyes infinitely greater, one than which no other could seem more formidable, threatened them. Bradford adds: —

> That which was more lámentable, and of all sorowes most heavie to be borne, was that many of their children, by these occasions, and yᵉ great licentiousnes of youth in yᵗ countrie, and yᵉ manifold temptations of the place, were drawne away by evill examples into extravagante & dangerous courses, getting yᵉ raines off their neks, & departing from their parents. Some became souldiers, others tooke upon them farr viages by sea, and other some worse courses, tending to dissolutenes & the danger of their soules, to yᵉ great greefe of their parents and dishonour of God. So that they saw their posteritie would be in danger to degenerate & be corrupted.

These hardships — poverty, oppressive toil, the perils of their children, the failure of the company to grow as had been hoped, and the probability of its ultimate extinction — convinced them that they had not yet found a proper home. The existing twelve years' truce between the

Dutch and the Spaniards also was about to expire, — in 1621, — so that to remain might mean to incur all the horrors of war. Moreover, they had a larger purpose than merely to provide for themselves. They had come from England glowing with missionary zeal. They had hoped to maintain their existence as a body in Holland so as to set the example of a godly community and a pure church, and, this hope failing, the same motive impelled them to look to more distant lands for some opportunity to live, labor, and testify for God. Says Bradford : —

> Lastly (and which was not least,) a great hope & inward zeall they had of laying some good foundation, or at least to make some way therunto, for ye propagating & advancing ye gospell of ye kingdom of Christ in those remote parts of ye world; yea, though they should be but even as stepping-stones unto others for ye performing of so great a work.

Slowly their new purpose took definite shape. In spite of their conviction of its expediency and even necessity, the proposed change involved the gravest consequences, as they fully understood. It might lead them to success, but it was almost equally likely to prove their ruin, as their sad history for several subsequent years will be found to show. Many objections had to be considered, and grave practical hindrances appeared. The question whither to move was most difficult to be answered. Some proposed Guiana, because of its known fertility. But its hot climate and the danger of annoyance by the Spaniards deterred them from going thither. Others favored Virginia, where Englishmen already had established the feeble Jamestown settlement.

They finally decided to go somewhere in Virginia, but to establish an independent colony of their own, in order to avoid as much as possible the interference of the English ecclesiastical powers. So they sent Robert Cushman and John Carver over to London in the autumn of 1617 to obtain, if possible, the royal permission and to make arrangements with the Virginia Company, which owned Virginia under the king. But King James was almost as bitter against them as ever and could only be brought to say that if they behaved peaceably he would not interfere.[3] All sanction of the undertaking he refused. The Virginia Company was favorable, however, being eager to have its territory settled, and offered to grant a liberal charter. With this report the envoys returned.

The history of the negotiations need not be related here in full. They were not completed until the late spring or early summer of 1620. Brewster also was sent to London to aid in making arrangements, and it is uncertain whether he returned to Leyden or remained in England until the emigrants arrived there on their way to America.[4] The council of the Virginia Company opposed them after all, for ecclesiastical reasons, and explanations had to be made. Friends failed and merchants betrayed them, and annoyances of various other sorts occurred. Meanwhile, certain Dutch acquaintances urged them to settle in Zeland or at New Amsterdam, now New York, and applied through the proper officials to the Dutch States General, or national legislature, for the granting of conditions. But the scheme came to nothing, although it seems to have been considered with some attention by the Pilgrims. At last one Thomas Weston and other London merchants and speculators made them offers of sufficient aid, and they made ready to depart from Holland.

Some could not go, nor could transportation for all be obtained. So the company was divided into two parts, the majority remaining. When the question arose how their ecclesiastical organization was to be affected by the division, it was decided that the majority should follow the minority to America as soon as possible, that each of the two portions of the church should be considered an absolute church by itself meanwhile, and that members should be interchanged, upon occasion, without formalities. Robinson, partly because it was the majority which remained and partly for other reasons, stayed behind, but it was determined that Brewster should go. Then preparations were hastened. Only a very few weeks, probably not more than three or four, intervened between their final decision to go, as described, and their setting out. Those who were to emigrate sold what property they had in Leyden and made a common purse. A small vessel, the Speedwell, was bought both for the voyage and for subsequent use in America; and a larger ship, the Mayflower, was hired in London for the voyage only.

Finally, after a day of solemn fasting and prayer, on which Robinson preached an impressive sermon from Ezra 8 : 21, they bade farewell to Leyden.

They lefte y^t goodly & pleasante citie, which had been ther resting-place near 12 years; but they knew they were pilgrims, & looked not much on those things, but lift up their eyes to yᵉ heavens, their dearest cuntrie, and quieted their spirits.

They journeyed over to Delfshaven, fourteen miles distant, accompanied by most of their friends, and on the next day — July 22, 1620 — they set sail. Bradford's account of the parting is too touching to be omitted :—

That night was spent with little sleepe by yᵉ most, but with freindly entertainmente & christian discourse and other reall expressions of true christian love. The next day, the wind being faire they wente aborde, and their freinds with them, where truly dolfull was yᵉ sight of that sade and mournfull parting; to see what sighs and sobbs and praires did sound amongst them, what tears did gush from every eye, & pithy speeches peirst each harte; that sundry of yᵉ Dutch strangers yᵗ stood on yᵉ key as spectators, could not refraine from tears. Yet comfortable & sweete it was to see shuch lively and true expressions of dear & unfained love. But yᵉ tide (which stays for no man) caling them away yᵗ were thus loath to departe, their Revēᵈ pastor falling downe on his knees, (and they all with him,) with watrie cheeks comended them with most fervente praiers to the Lord and his blessing. And then with mutuall imbrases and many tears, they tooke their leaves one of an other; which proved to be ye last leave to many of them.

They had a short and pleasant voyage to Southampton, where they found the Mayflower awaiting them.

CHAPTER XIV.

THE VOYAGE TO AMERICA.

THEY received a hearty welcome at Southampton from "all the rest of their company," by which is meant the few whom they had sent over beforehand to consummate arrangements, and also a number of their fellow Separatists, who never had joined them in Holland, but had determined to accompany them to America and were awaiting them at Southampton. A letter from Robert Cushman to John Carver implies that the whole number of intending emigrants was about a hundred and fifty.[1] These additions to their company and the assurances of sympathy which they received must have been most encouraging. But they found themselves in financial difficulties at once. Before the departure from Leyden, while communication between the English section of the party and that in Leyden had been maintained by letters and occasional messengers, one Christopher Martin from Billerica, in Essex, had been chosen to represent the English element in conjunction with Brewster, Cushman, and Carver, who had been sent to London in behalf of the Leyden contingent. Owing to some carelessness or misunderstanding on the part of these agents — Cushman seems to have been chiefly at fault — insufficient energy had been displayed and debts had been incurred.

The niggardly Weston also had demanded that the conditions originally drawn up between the colonists and the merchants who were helping to fit them out be altered, and Cushman had taken it upon himself to agree in behalf of the emigrants to a proposed equal division, between the settlers and the merchants, of the whole property in the colony at the end of seven years after its settlement, which was unfair to the former and which they now, upon learning of it, at first very properly objected to indorse. They claimed that the houses and improved lands, their gardens and home lots, upon which they would have expended special pains for the sake of their necessary comfort, ought to belong to them at the end of the seven years and not be liable to fall into the hands of the London merchants. They also insisted that each colonist should be allowed to work for himself two days in each week and not be compelled to labor all six days for the company. These positions certainly seem reasonable, and, in any case, the colonists were not bound by Cushman's unauthorized acceptance in their behalf of other conditions. But Weston " was much offended, and tould them, they must then locke to stand on their owne leggs," and they sailed finally without having signed the disputed contract.

They were forced to sell some of their

provisions in order to pay their debts, and reduced themselves to "great extremities, scarce haveing any butter, no oyle, not a sole to mend a shoe, nor every man a sword to his side, wanting many muskets, much armoure, &c." In the end, however, their affairs were settled and they were ready to depart. They were called together, a wise and loving letter from Robinson, which appears to have been written on or about July 27 and to have followed them from Leyden, was read, and they elected a governor and two or three assistants for each vessel, to have in charge their order and comfort on the voyage. At last, on August 15, they sailed from Southampton.

Fairly afloat and headed westward they must have thought that now their hindrances were ended. But this was not true. The Speedwell began to leak, and Mr. Reinolds, her captain, declared that repairs were unavoidable. So both ships were headed about and, probably on

August 23, they put in at Dartmouth, that picturesque little Devonshire harbor whence so many privateering or exploring expeditions had gone forth in former days. Here the Speedwell was overhauled at considerable cost, which they could only with difficulty afford, and while a fair wind blew, of which they were eager to take advantage. On September 2, they set sail once more.

But after they had proceeded about three hundred miles the leaks reopened and again both ships put back, this time to Plymouth. Of course all this additional voyaging was not only exceedingly disheartening but it also made heavy inroads upon their provisions, which at the best were none too abundant for the unknown future. It was finally decided to abandon the Speedwell as unfit for the proposed voyage and to transfer to the Mayflower as many of her passengers and stores as could be accommodated. So another painful parting occurred, and at least twenty persons, and probably more, including Robert Cushman, whose heart had failed,[2] and his family, went back to London in the Speedwell. It appeared later that there had been nothing really the matter with this vessel, but that she deliberately had been oversparred and caused to carry too much sail in order to force her to strain and leak, the reason being that the captain and crew, who had been hired to stay a year with the colony, wished to avoid the fulfilment of this pledge.[3] As soon as she was refitted in her former trim she ceased to leak and long did good service. One hundred and two persons remained in the Pilgrim company.

It is probable, however, that this company actually was no weaker for this sifting which it experienced. Most of those who were left behind would have proved unequal to the severe demands of the early life of the colony. Says Bradford : —

Those that went bak were for the most parte such as were willing so to doe, either out of some discontente, or feare they conceived of yᵉ ill success of yᵉ vioage, seeing so many croses befale, & the year time so farr spente; but others, in regarde of their own weaknes, and charge of many yonge children, were thought least usefull, and most unfite to bear yᵉ brunte of this hard adventure; unto which worke of God, and judgmente of their brethern, they were contented to submite.

Yet in any case, and especially happening as it did, this diminution of the little company must have been acutely depressing. Once more, on September 16, the Mayflower put to sea, this time to accomplish her errand.

No picture of this famous vessel is known to exist. Some idea of her appearance can be obtained by the study of other vessels of her time, as shown in old maps and paintings, but they necessarily are only examples of what she may have been. It is certain that she now would be considered a very slow and clumsy craft. Undoubtedly she was shorter than many American coasting schooners of to-day and was much less graceful in her lines than the most old-fashioned ones among them. Doubtless she had a blunt, full bow and stern, each of which was built up much higher than is now customary, and probably she was of a considerably broader beam in proportion to her length than would be true at present. This shape lessened her speed but of course added largely to her carrying capacity. Whether she had two masts or three is not known. Probably her bowsprit pointed upward much higher than that of any modern ship, and she may have had a short mast rising almost from her very stem. Many a vessel of her period carried a small sail under or uplifted on a short mast upon the outer end of the bowsprit, in order to aid in going about, and in some imaginary pictures of the Mayflower she has been given one. Doubtless she was square-rigged. Internally she probably differed less from modern vessels, although lacking many of their conveniences. But at her best she must have been a confined and disagreeable abode for her one hundred and twenty-five to fifty inmates during their nine weeks' voyage.

At first she had a fair wind which continued for a number of days, so that she made good progress, and ordinary seasickness was the only drawback to the comfort of the passengers. But in due time they encountered foul weather and fierce storms. The upper works of the ship became leaky enough to render her uncomfortable, and one of her main beams amidships somehow became sprung and also cracked. There was sufficient appearance of danger to cause a conference of the ship's officers and the leading passengers about the advisability of abandoning the whole undertaking and returning finally. But examination showed the ship to be stanch below the water line, and by the aid of a great iron jackscrew, which the Pilgrims had on board, the defective beam was forced back into place and braced. So they held on their course although compelled by the violent gales to lie to for days at a time.

On one occasion a young man of the Pilgrim company, John Howland, had a narrow escape from drowning. He was thrown overboard by a lurch of the ship, but caught hold of a loose topsail halyard and held on until he could be dragged on board again. Those who have made a westward Atlantic voyage in the teeth of autumnal or winter storms and have seen the largest and stanchest modern steamers unable, as they sometimes are, to make any headway for many hours at a time can imagine the distress and fear of the company on the little Mayflower. On November 16, three days before they made land, William Butten, a servant of Samuel Fuller, died, and doubtless was buried in the sea. This death was offset, however, by the birth of a son, who was named Oceanus, to Stephen Hopkins.

The longest voyages end, however, and on November 19,[4] more than nine weary weeks after leaving Plymouth, they made Cape Cod. It is no wonder that, as Bradford says, "they were not a little joyfull." It was their wish to settle on or near the Hudson River, so they stood away towards the south to clear the cape. But they soon found themselves among dangerous shoals, probably off the present towns of Eastham and Orleans,[5] and were glad to go about and return to Cape Cod. Doubling the end of the cape, they anchored at last, on November 21, sixty-six days out from England, in the calm and spacious harbor of what is now Provincetown. Then, characteristically,

> they fell upon their knees & blessed ye God of heaven, who had brought them over ye vast & furious ocean, and delivered them from all ye periles & miseries thereof, againe to set their feete on ye firme and stable earth, their proper elemente.

After all their tribulations they had reached America in safety. Fortunately they could not foresee the new perils and bitter distresses which they soon were to be called upon to face, or they would have been sorely tempted to return without disembarking.

CHAPTER XV.

OTHER PILGRIM LEADERS AND THEIR COMPACT.

IN proportion to its numbers the colony was richly endowed with able leaders, and without them it must have failed utterly and speedily. Mention has been made already of Robinson, who, more than any one else, although he remained in Leyden, gave to it its abiding moral and spiritual impulse; of Brewster, its original principal, wise and experienced, the patron, so to speak, of the enterprise; and of Bradford, its thoughtful scholar, careful historian, and prudent, energetic man of affairs. It remains to describe several of their almost equally efficient coadjutors.

For instance, there was the discreet and trusted John Carver,[1] their first governor He was one of the company in Leyden, where he was a deacon in their church, but when and whence he joined them is unrecorded. There is no evidence that he was one of them before they reached Leyden, and probably he went over to them there from England. He was sufficiently prominent among them to be sent back to England in 1617 with Robert Cushman, to make arrangements for the proposed emigration to America, and he returned to Leyden in the same year and later was sent once more on the same errand. Apparently he left Holland finally before the others and joined them again at Southampton. Robinson sent to him from Leyden, after the departure of the emigrants, a special personal letter of confidence and affection, together with one addressed to the whole company. He was accompanied to America in the Mayflower by his wife, Catherine, by a maid-servant, Desire Minter, and by two menservants and two lads, which little retinue probably implies that he was a man of more substance than most of the others. He was chosen to be the first governor of the colony before they landed, and was reelected in the spring of 1621, but immediately afterwards he received what seems to have been a sunstroke and soon died, and was buried with such official honors as the feeble company was able to pay. He was greatly missed, and Bradford, who was made governor in his place, wrote home about him: "His care and pains was so great for ye commone good, both ours and yours, as that therwith (it is thought) he oppressed him selfe and shortened his days; of whose loss we cannot sufficiently complaine." His wife survived him only a few weeks.

Then there was Edward Winslow,[2] who properly may be termed their diplomatist. He had been born at Droitwich, October 28, 1594, of a prominent family, and he is said to have made the tour of Europe while yet young, a fact then sufficiently unusual to imply almost certainly that his parents were not only of superior social position but also comparatively wealthy. But in 1617 he joined the Pilgrims in Leyden, the records of which city declare him to have been a printer there and to have come from London. That he was obliged to support himself thus indicates that he had cut loose from or had been cast off by his family, probably because of his Separatist opinions. On May 17, 1618,[3] he was married to Elizabeth Barker, who, with a maid and two men servants, accompanied him in the Mayflower. His wife soon died and on May 22, 1621, he was married again to Susanna White. He was prominent in treating with the Indians and establishing the colony and was its governor during several years.

He also was sent to England repeatedly in its behalf and in 1635 he was imprisoned in London for several months, at the instance of Archbishop Laud, for having presumed to teach in the church, although only a layman, and for having as a magistrate performed the marriage ceremony. In 1649 he was one of the founders in England of a corporation formed for the propagation of the gospel among the Indians of New England, and he also was one of three commissioners appointed in 1654 by Cromwell to determine the value of certain English ships destroyed by the king of Denmark. Furthermore in 1655 he was the chief of the three commissioners who accompanied the English naval expedition to Hispaniola, commanded by Admiral Penn and General Venable. Much of his later life seems to have been spent in England and in positions of honor, but his loyalty to the Plymouth Colony never diminished. He appears to have been the only member of the Pilgrim company who gained an eminence recognized at the time in England as conspicuous. He died at sea between St. Domingo and Jamaica, on May 8, 1655. In addition to his other valuable services he was an author of repute. He wrote a large portion of *Mourt's Relation* and several entire works: *Hypocrisie Vnmasked; Good News from New England; A brief Narrative of the True Grounds or Cause of the first Planting of New England; New England's Salamander;* etc.

Another Pilgrim, and one whom Longfellow has rendered one of the most widely known, was Miles Standish,[4] their foremost man in military matters. This stout-hearted soldier, whom the wily and cruel Indians could neither outwit nor frighten, and who, although short in stature, was a formidable opponent, is supposed to have been born of a good family at Duxbury Hall, near Chorley, in 1584. He is said to have been heir to a large estate but somehow was deprived of it. On reaching manhood he served as a soldier in the Low Countries, where he somehow fell in with the Pilgrims and joined them, although without uniting with their church. His wife, Rose, came over with him in the Mayflower but soon after died. Whether there is any basis for the tradition in regard to his attempt to woo Priscilla Mullins by proxy — John Alden, whom she chose to marry, acting as Standish's agent and receiving from her an intimation to substitute the part of principal for that of representative — is uncertain. The poet has made the tradition pleasantly familiar at any rate. Whether it be true or not, Standish did not break his heart over the matter, for in 1623 he was married again to Barbara ———, a recent arrival in the colony whose surname is not on record. He was the mainstay of the colonists during their difficulties with the Indians and with the troublesome settlers at Merry Mount, and he was employed often and otherwise in the public service. In 1625 he too was sent to England for the colony. About 1631 he settled on what has since been called Captain's Hill, in Duxbury, and died there on October 13, 1656. He was a sturdy, rugged character, in some respects quite unlike most of his fellow Pilgrims, but he was deservedly beloved and trusted by them.

Their most active man in commercial affairs was Isaac Allerton,[5] who joined them, from London, in Leyden, where he was a tailor. On November 4, 1611, he was married there to Mary Norris, and he became a citizen of Leyden on February 7, 1614. He brought with him on the Mayflower his wife, three children, and a boy, but his wife soon died, and he married William Brewster's daughter, Fear, and after her death in 1633 he married a third wife. Apparently he soon became the wealthiest man in the colony and he was sent to England several times on its business. But as the severity of the conditions of life at Plymouth gradually abated and as opportunities for accumulation increased, his money-making passion got the better of his nobler nature, as so often happens, and he became more strenuous to promote his own prosperity than that of the colony, and did not always obey his instructions. At last he mismanaged their funds so suspiciously, that in 1631 the Plymouth church felt compelled to discipline him for his shortcomings, and the next year he left the colony. After various wanderings he reached New Haven, where in 1659 he died insolvent, the not unusual fate of such men. He was almost the only one of the original Pilgrim body, and the only one eminent among them, who failed to maintain a good repute, and for a number of years he was one of the most active and useful of the company.

Mention also should be made here of Samuel Fuller,[6] the good physician of the colony. He is believed to have lived for a time in London before joining the Pilgrims in Leyden. There he was a deacon in the church, and he held the same office after they had reached Plymouth. He also was one of the governor's assistants in 1631. Like others of the company he was married several times, first to Alice

Glascock, then to Agnes Carpenter, and after her death to Bridget Lee, to whom he was united in Leyden in 1617, and who, with their child, remained there until 1623, when she came over in the Anne and rejoined him. He was one of their most trusted members, and in 1629, when an epidemic of "scurvy and malignant distemper" had broken out in the new colony at Salem, and Endicott had sent to Plymouth for help, he hastened thither and rendered most acceptable aid. It also was largely due to his explanations at this time of the polity of the Pilgrim church that the misunderstandings and prejudices which leading men at Salem entertained in regard to it were removed. He died in 1633 on July 30, and his will, which was proved on October 28, is said to be the earliest on record in the colony.

The only other Pilgrim whom it is important to mention in this connection is John Alden.[7] He was a young Englishman who joined the emigrants, to serve them as a cooper, at Southampton. After reaching Plymouth in America, he married Priscilla Mullins. He was one of the most efficient and prominent men in the colony until his death, in 1687, and left a large family, from whom many descendants have sprung.

We turn now to the famous Mayflower compact. The orderly and religious character of the men who have just been described and their fellow Pilgrims certainly needs no demonstration. But even among the best of men a formal agreement determining authority always is wise, if only because of its convenience. Moreover, the Mayflower company, as it finally was composed, included some who were not actual members of their body. A number of sailors or adventurers appear to have made the voyage with them, who were minded to remain, and whose lack of religious purpose was tolerated because of their fewness and of the value of every able-bodied man; and even before a landing had been made it became evident that some of these men might make trouble unless restrained. Bradford speaks of

> yᵉ discontented & mutinous speeches that some of the strangers amongst them had let fall from them in yᵉ ship — That when they came a shore they would use their owne libertie; for none had power to comand them.[8]

In order to nip any such factious spirit in the bud, it was therefore decided that formal action was necessary. Bradford, in that portion of *Mourt's Relation* which he wrote, says : —

> This day before we came to harbour, obseruing some not well affected to vnitie and concord, but gaue some appearance of faction, it was thought good there should be an association and agreement, that we should combine together in one body, and to submit to such government and governours, as we should by common consent agree to make and chose, and set our hands to this that followes word for word.[9]

So they drew up and signed their renowned compact, a document of great and permanent significance. It was this : —

In the name of God, Amen. We whose names are vnderwritten, the loyall Subiects of our dread soveraigne Lord King IAMES, by the grace of God of Great *Britaine, France,* and *Ireland* King, Defender of the Faith, &c.
Having vnder-taken for the glory of God, and advancement of the Christian Faith, and honour of our King and Countrey, a Voyage to plant the first Colony in the Northerne parts of VIRGINIA, doe by these presents solemnly & mutually in the presence of *God* and one of another, covenant, and combine our selues together into a civill body politike, for our better ordering and preservation, and furtherance of the ends aforesaid ; and by vertue hereof to enact, constitute and frame such just and equall Lawes, Ordinances, acts, constitutions, offices from time to time, as shall be thought most meet and convenient for the generall good of the Colony: vnto which we promise all due submission and obedience. In witnesse whereof we haue here-vnder subscribed our names, *Cape Cod,* 11. of *November,* in the yeare of the raigne of our soveraigne Lord King IAMES, of *England, France* and *Ireland* 18. and of *Scotland* 54. *Anno Domini* 1620.

John Carver.	Edward Fuller.
William Bradford.	John Turner.
Edward Winslow.	Francis Eaton.
William Brewster.	James Chilton.
Isaac Allerton.	John Crackstone.
Miles Standish.	John Billington.
John Alden.	Moses Fletcher.
Samuel Fuller.	John Goodman.
Christopher Martin.	Digory Priest.
William Mullins.	Thomas Williams.
William White.	Gilbert Winslow.
Richard Warren.	Edmond Margeson.
John Howland.	Peter Brown.
Stephen Hopkins.	Richard Britteridge.
Edward Tilley.	George Soule.
John Tilley.	Richard Clark.
Francis Cook.	Richard Gardiner.
Thomas Rogers.	John Allerton.
Thomas Tinker.	Thomas English.
John Ridgdale.	Edward Doten.
	Edward Leister.[10]

Having thus organized themselves into a body politic, and having elected John Carver their first governor, they then set about exploring the country which, after so many hardships, they had reached.

CHAPTER XVI.

FIRST EXPLORATIONS.

IT was on Saturday, November 21, 1620, — they dated it November 11, because they used the old style, — that the Pilgrims cast anchor in Provincetown harbor, and drew up and signed their civil compact. On the same day they sent their first party ashore for wood and fresh water, and the latter, at least, they must by this time have come to desire greatly. Before their eyes lay an agreeable scene, "a good harbour and pleasant Bay, circled round, except in the entrance, which is about foure miles ouer from land to land, compassed about to the very Sea with Okes, Pines, Iuniper, Sassafras, and other sweet wood,"[1] and this statement that the end of Cape Cod ever was thus thickly wooded may be a surprise to many of those who are familiar with it now. The name "Wood End" still is applied to it occasionally. But in other respects the prospect which lay before them was dreary indeed. Says Bradford : —

> They had now no freinds to wellcome them, nor inns to entertaine or refresh their weather-beaten bodys, no houses or much less townes to repaire too, to seeke for succoure. It is recorded in scripture as a mercie to ye apostle & his shipwraked company, y^t the barbarians shewed them no smale kindnes in refreshing them, but these savage barbarians, when they mette with them (as after will appeare) were readier to fill their sids full of arrows then otherwise. And for ye season it was winter, and they that know ye winters of y^t cuntrie know them to be sharp & violent, & subjecte to cruell & feirce stormes, deangerous to travill to known places, much more to serch an unknown coast. Besids, what could they see but a hidious & desolate wilderness, full of wild beasts & willd men? and what multituds ther might be of them they knew not.[2]

Even the joy of reaching land hardly can have afforded them more than partial and temporary satisfaction.

First Explorations.

It was of vital importance, of course, to find a suitable place of settlement speedily. So having passed Sunday quietly on board ship, and having landed some of the company on Monday long enough to wash clothes, it was determined to send out an exploring party. Their largest boat, the shallop, had been injured during the voyage and could not be used until repaired. But on Wednesday, November 25, they sent off sixteen men by land under Captain Standish to learn what they could of the country and its inhabitants.[3] They were absent two days, camping at night with fires and sentries. They saw five or six natives and a dog, but could not get near enough for intercourse. They explored the country for perhaps a dozen miles through the woods or along the shore and discovered some springs in what is now Truro. They saw a deer and traversed land where corn had been raised by the Indians and also found some heaps of corn buried in the ground. Moreover they came upon the ruins of a house and of what seemed to have been a small fort, as well as a bow, arrows, a large kettle, and two canoes, but they met no more inhabitants.

They carried away the corn, intending to pay for it should they discover the owners, and returned safely to the Mayflower, William Bradford, one of the party, having had a narrow escape from injury on the way by being caught in a trap set by the Indians for deer. The country seemed to abound in wild game, for they saw considerable flocks of ducks and geese and some partridges. They also saw more deer but could not kill any. They had traveled as far as the Pamet River, but had accomplished little. They must have formed a procession at once picturesque and pathetic, as they waded heavily through the soft sand of the seashore or pushed their way through the straggling underbrush of the forest, — which was so stubborn that they said "it tore our very armor to pieces," — obliged to be ever on the watch against sudden attack from hidden human foes or savage wild beasts and equally alert to allow no important feature of the country to escape their critical observation.

For the next few days they were busy repairing the shallop, but on December 7 they sent out a larger exploring party in her and the long boat under charge of Master Jones, the captain of the Mayflower.[4] They experienced bitter cold with high winds and snow, but coasted alongshore and also penetrated the country somewhat farther than before. They shot some geese and ducks, discovered some Indian graves and two empty wigwams, found more corn, together with some wheat and beans, as well as a bottle of oil, and rejoined the ship on December 10. During their absence Peregrine White had been born, the first child born to any of them in America.

They were not favorably impressed with

the fitness of the region for settlement, yet they weighed the matter well before deciding to continue their explorations. It might easily be that to go further would mean to fare worse at last. Some desired to remain where they were, urging that they had a good anchorage for boats, although the bay was so shoal in that part that the Mayflower had to lie at an inconvenient distance from the shore; that the soil was good for corn and they had found enough — some ten bushels — for seed; that the fishing promised to be excellent; that the region seemed healthy, secure and defensible; and that further investigation of the country, while it would use up provisions and would be necessarily in the teeth of bitter weather, might accomplish nothing. Moreover, Captain Jones and his crew were eager to land the company and set sail for home as soon as possible. But others raised objections, chiefly relating to the difficulty of obtaining water where they were, and it was proposed to try to find Agawam, the present Ipswich, of which they had heard. Finally it was determined to send out one more exploring party and await results. Meanwhile, Francis,[5] a scapegrace son of John Billington, caused a great excitement by firing a fowling-piece in the cabin, in which some powder was stored, and nearly blowing up the ship.

On Wednesday, December 16, the third and last party set forth.[6] It consisted of twelve Pilgrims, apparently volunteers, under Standish, together with six of the ship's officers and crew. They went in the shallop and the first day they proceeded as far as the present Eastham and saw some Indians at a distance on the shore, cutting up a "Grampus." The next day they held on their course toward the modern Wellfleet and found a small abandoned Indian village. That night, however, they were sharply attacked by Indians but escaped harm. The day following, Friday, December 18, they followed the coast around to the west and north and somehow, probably because it rained and snowed severely, passed the entrance to Barnstable Bay without seeing it. But after a hard battle with the gale, breaking both mast and rudder and almost being wrecked upon a lee shore, in the evening they ran into Plymouth Bay and anchored under the shelter of Clark's Island, which is said to have been thus named because one Clarke, a master's mate and pilot of the Mayflower, was first of the party to set foot upon it. They landed on Saturday and explored the place and rested there quietly on Sunday, and on Monday, December 21 — now called Forefathers' Day in memory of that event — they set foot on the main shore, where Plymouth now is, and made some examination of the region. They were pleased with it, and doubtless on the next day returned to the Mayflower, agreeing to recommend the spot as the site of the proposed settlement. But the satisfaction of William

PLYMOUTH BAY FROM BURIAL HILL, 1846.

First Explorations. 197

Bradford, who was one of the party, over its success was overshadowed upon its return, for he learned that on the day after their departure his wife, Dorothy, had fallen overboard and been drowned.

The Mayflower set sail from Provincetown on Christmas Day and stood over toward Plymouth, but could not make harbor until the day following, on which at last she dropped anchor inside of the bay, and the Pilgrims had reached their new home. They devoted a day or two more to examination of the immediate neighborhood in order to determine which of several spots would be most advantageous for their purpose, and finally, on Wednesday, December 30, they selected their now famous abiding-place. It is interesting to note how it impressed Bradford. He says : —

> After our landing and viewing of the places, so well as we could we came to a conclusion, by most voyces, to set on the maine Land, on the first place, on an high ground, where there is a great deale of

Land cleared, and hath beene planted with Corne three or four yeares agoe, and there is a very sweet brooke runnes vnder the hill side, and many delicate springs of as good water as can be drunke, and where we may harbour our Shallops and Boates exceeding well, and in this brooke much good fish in their seasons: on the further side of the river also much Corne ground cleared, in one field is a great hill, on which wee poynt to make a platforme, and plant our Ordinance, which will command all round about, from thence we may see into the *Bay*, and farre into the Sea, and we may see thence *Cape Cod:* our greatest labour will be fetching of our wood, which is halfe a quarter of an English myle, but there is enough so farre off; what people inhabite here we yet know not, for as yet we haue seene none.[7]

Even in the bleak winter the spot evidently had genuine attractions and promised reasonable safety, convenience, and comfort. The cause of the dearth of a native population, as they learned before many months, was the fact that nearly all the Indians thereabouts had died of an epidemic,[8] which the Pilgrims called the plague, about four years previous, the way thus having been cleared providentially for the comparatively unopposed settlement of the Mayflower colony. Nevertheless, not yet being aware of this and having already receivēd clear proofs of the reluctance of the natives to welcome them and even of active hostility towards them, they naturally were afraid of being attacked and felt compelled to be continually on their guard.

CHAPTER XVII.

THE BEGINNING OF THE COLONY.

IT was now midwinter and the region presented its least winsome aspect, but their general impressions continued favorable as their knowledge of the locality increased, and neither any regret because of their decision not to settle on the end of Cape Cod nor any desire to try their fortune elsewhere is recorded. Preliminary explorations made near Plymouth were confined almost wholly to Clark's Island and the shores of the bay. No one ventured far inland for fear of attack by Indians, but, so far as they went, they saw no inhabitants. They found the country "goodly," having a rich soil and with disused cornfields and ample forests, with "4. or 5. small running brookes of very sweet fresh water . . . the best water that ever we drunke," and the bay "a most hopefull place," with "innumerable store of fowl, and excellent good, and cannot be but of fish in their seasons," with "abundance of Musles, the greatest & best that ever we saw," and "Crabs and Lobsters, in their time infinite." Their choice being thus confirmed, they finally, after prayer for divine direction, chose a favorable spot for building.

This decision was made on Wednesday, December 30, and some of the company camped on shore that night.[1] But the hardships of the season at once befell them afresh. A severe storm prevented work and even forbade communication between ship and shore, until Saturday, January 2, 1621, when as many of them as could went on shore and "felled and carried tymber, to provide themselves stuffe for building." It was necessary, of course, to put up some sort of dwellings and, in order to make as few houses as possible serve their purpose at first, they assigned the unmarried men to the different families, thus reducing the number of houses to be built to nineteen, which, as there were but eighteen married couples, apparently includes, as Bradford describes it, "the common house, in which for the first, we made our Rendevous,"[2] a building which was erected first of all in order to shelter the workers, the balance of the company continuing on the Mayflower.

They also determined to form a street with houses upon each side, the present Leyden Street, and they staked out the land in plots. The areas of these inclosures were proportioned to the sizes of the families, "to every person half a pole in breadth, and three in length." This gave to Carver's household, for example, in which were eight persons, a lot of sixty-six feet by forty-nine and a half feet. This seems a small allowance for so numerous a family, especially in view of the abundance of land; and Bradford touchingly suggests the trials which they were experiencing in giving the reason of it. He says : —

> We thought this proportion was large enough at the first, for houses and gardens, to impale them round, considering the weaknes of our people, many of them growing ill with coldes, for our former Discoveries in frost and stormes, and the wading at Cape *Cod* had brought much weakeness amongst us, which increased so every day more and more, and after was the cause of many of their deaths.

It is plain that they already had begun to suffer seriously and generally from their inevitable exposures, and one of the earliest buildings completed had to be devoted to the uses of a hospital.

They assigned the different plots of land by lot. Then they set themselves as vigorously as they could in their enfeebled condition to the task of erecting their houses. By January 4 they were hard at work upon the "common house." It was only twenty feet square, but, says the historian, the "foule weather hindered vs much, this time of the yeare seldome

could wee work halfe the weeke." It was
an inclement New England winter,[3] and
to all who know by experience what this
means the few words of the record are full
of mournful significance. This building, so
important to their comfort and even safety,
rude and hurriedly constructed although
it was, was not finished until January
20 or later, and then a new peril began
to threaten. The thatched roof took fire
at least twice from sparks out of the
chimney and was burned, leaving only the
frame timbers. On one of these occasions
both Bradford and Carver were sick in
bed within, and, as a number of loaded
guns and apparently some gunpowder also
were stored there, they had a narrow
escape from being blown up. But no
harm was done except to the thatch, which
soon was replaced. The little village
came into visible existence by degrees,
and at last the whole company was disem-
barked in time to keep their first Sabbath
ashore together on January 31.

While at work upon their houses they did no exploring and did not often venture far away from the settlement, although once or twice some of them penetrated six or seven miles into the country. But upon one occasion John Goodman and Peter Brown, while cutting coarse grass and flags for use in thatching, saw a deer and, while pursuing it, managed to lose themselves without food and had a bitter experience walking up and down under a tree during "an extreame colde night" and in great fear of "Lyons roaring exceedingly," and it was late the next afternoon before they found their way back. The "Lyons" undoubtedly were wolves. Their companions naturally feared that they had been captured and possibly killed by Indians, of whom they all were in continual apprehension. For some weeks they saw none, but several times they discerned in the distance smoke and fires which could have been made only by Indians. At last, on February 10, some of them saw two savages in the distance, and on February 26 one of the company, having ventured a mile and a half away from the settlement after wild fowl, saw a dozen or more Indians pass the spot where he lay concealed, and Captain Standish and Francis Cook also had some tools stolen which they had left over night where they had been at work in the woods.

These occurrences naturally rendered the settlers additionally uneasy, so on February 27 they held a meeting to effect a military organization and chose Miles Standish captain. While this very meeting was in progress two savages appeared upon a neighboring hill, but ran away when an effort was made to parley with them. This led the Pilgrims to mount their cannon at once upon the hill near their houses, where they had planned to have a fortification. About a month afterwards, on March 26, — by an odd coincidence, which also occurred twice more a few days later, — while they were holding another meeting about military matters, an Indian walked in among them, who to their surprise accosted them in broken English. His name was Samoset, and he was chief of a tribe living in what is now Maine. He had met many English fishermen along the northern coast, had accompanied one of them to Cape Cod some six months before, and had remained in that part of the country. He proved to be friendly to the Pilgrims and served subsequently as an interpreter between them and the natives.

He remained over night and then was sent away with gifts. He returned the next day with five others and stayed three days, and the day following, April 1, returned again with Squanto, a native Indian who also spoke English, — having been formerly taken to England by Captain George Waymouth or Captain Thomas Hunt, — and announced that Massasoit, the Indian sagamore of that region, with his brother, Quadequina, and sixty others, sought an interview. This was felt to be an important event and it was treated with due respect. Edward Winslow was sent to greet them, a formal meeting was held with appropriate hospitalities, and a treaty of peace was agreed upon. Thus the colonists' fears of the natives were largely removed; and, as matters turned out, partly because of the comparatively small number of Indians in the nearer country and partly because of the uniform fair dealing of the Pilgrims with the natives, as well as of the firm and apparently fearless behavior of the former whenever the latter did venture upon an aggressive policy, the settlers thenceforth had only occasional and never very serious trouble from this source.

As the spring opened they were able to devote themselves more freely to completing their settlement. At the best, however, their case was hard and their prospect far from cheering. In addition to the ordinary severities and perils attending the establishing of a new colony, and their not yet finally allayed fear of the Indians, concerning atrocities at whose hands elsewhere they continued to hear now and then, they had encountered a far more cold and tempestuous winter than they were equipped to endure. There also had been disaffection among some, as had been feared when their compact had been drawn up, but this fortunately had been suppressed by firmness and fair dealing. Sickness, however, had been among them continually and death frequently. That they had not abandoned the colony in despair reveals their firmness of purpose and faith. The straits in which they had been at times cannot be described in any other words so faithfully as in those of Bradford himself.

That which was most sadd & lamentable was, that in 2. or 3. moneths time halfe of their company dyed, espetialy in Jan: & February, being ye depth of winter, and wanting houses & other comforts; being infected with ye scurvie & other diseases, which this long vioage & their inacomodate condition had brought upon them; so as ther dyed some times 2. or 3. of a day, in ye foresaid time; that of 100. & odd persons, scarce 50. remained.

They did not even dare to bury their dead openly, lest the Indians should detect the growing weakness of the colony, and were forced to inter them at night. They laid them not in the present burying-ground on the hill but probably on Cole's Hill, a mound or bluff lower and near the rock where they had landed, even smoothing the soil over them lest their graves should attract attention.[4] So greatly was the strength of the company reduced that

of these in ye time of most distres, ther was but 6. or 7. sound persons,[5] who, to their great comendations be it spoken, spared no pains, night nor day, but with abundance of toyle and hazard of their owne health, fetched them woode, made them fires, drest them meat, made their beads, washed their lothsome cloaths, cloathed & uncloathed them; in a word, did all ye homly & necessarie offices for them wch dainty & quesie stomacks cannot endure to hear named; and all this willingly and cherfully, without any grudging in ye least, shewing herein their true love unto their freinds & bretheren.

Truly their trials after gaining their spiritual liberty were equal to those which they had undergone during their long endeavor to obtain it.

CHAPTER XVIII.

THE FURTHER HISTORY OF THE FIRST YEAR.

AS the spring season came on, the forlorn condition of the colony slowly began to mend. Warmer weather brought them both health and encouragement.

It pleased God the mortalitie begane to cease amongst them, and ye sick and lame recovered apace, which put as it were new life into them; though they had borne their sadd affliction with much patience & contentednes.[1]

On April 2 the civil organization was completed and John Carver was reëlected governor for a year. After his death about a fortnight later William Bradford was chosen in his place, and as Bradford had not yet recovered wholly from a dangerous illness Isaac Allerton was chosen his assistant. The two were reëlected annually afterward for some years. The attention of the colony naturally was directed at once to planting the crops for the year, and in this work they found the Indian, Squanto, a great help. The corn which they had discovered at various times and places had been kept carefully for seed, and now Squanto taught them how to manure it with fish and plant it, and how to tend it after it began to grow. He also instructed them as to the season for fish in the neighboring brooks and how to capture them, and where other kinds of provisions could be found. But for his aid they might have come to famine, for the English seed, wheat, peas, etc., which they had brought with them, finally proved fruitless, and the corn turned out to be their mainstay.

Early in April, on or about the fifth, the Mayflower set sail for England. The unintended prolongation of her stay at Plymouth had been due at first to the extreme difficulty of rendering the colony habitable and later to the death or grave illness of many of the crew. Apparently, too, the authorities of the colony, although determined not to abandon the enterprise needlessly, had felt at one time, when matters were at the worst, that it might become necessary for them all to return.

 The Govr & cheefe of them, seeing so many dye, and fall downe sick dayly, thought it no wisdom to send away the ship, their condition considered, and ye danger they stood in from ye Indeans, till they could procure some shelter; . . . The m^r and seamen likewise, though before they hasted ye pasengers a shore to be goone, now many of their men being dead, & of ye ablest of them, . . . and of ye rest many lay sick & weake, ye m^r. durst not put to sea, till he saw his men begine to recover, and ye hart of winter over.

But by April matters looked brighter and the ship sailed for home. Then, at last, as her topsails sunk below the eastern horizon, the Pilgrims must have realized with a new solemnity that they were committed irrevocably to their chosen work.

Her departure gave them their first opportunity of reporting their progress to their friends left behind in England and Holland. Their letters, if now in existence, would be worth more than their weight in gold. With what sadness the writers must have recounted for the eyes which they knew would read their pages so eagerly the distressing story of their hardships and perils on sea and land, and especially the long list of the already dead! Yet we may be sure that they also wrote in brave and hopeful words, emphasizing the promising features of the colony and bearing witness, and in no merely formal terms, to their unshaken trust in the Divine love and care.

A prominent event which soon followed was the wedding of Edward Winslow and Susannah White. It took place on May 22 and was the first to occur among them. Winslow was a widower, his former wife,

Elizabeth, having died as recently as March 24, and Mrs. White's first husband, William, also had died no earlier than February 21. Probably the brevity of the interval between their respective bereavements and their marriage was due very largely, if not wholly, to the peculiar conditions of the young colony, in which family relations were felt to be much more advantageous than single life. The ceremony doubtless was very simple and unattended by any special festivities. It was civil in character and probably was performed by Governor Bradford as their magistrate. There was no minister among them,[2] and if there had been their views at that time did not allow them to make use of his services on such an occasion. Says Bradford : —

May 12. was ye first mariage in this place, which, according to ye laudable custome of ye Low-Cuntries, in which they had lived, was thought most requisite to be performed by the magistrate, as being a civill thing, upon which many questions aboute inheritances doe depende, with other things most proper to their cognizans, and most consonante to yͤ scripturs, Ruth 4. and no wher found in yͤ gospell to be layed on yͤ ministers as a part of their office.

There is no record beyond this concerning the occurrence and they were in too depressed and needy a state to make much ado over it, even if in other circumstances they would have been disposed to do so.

In the course of the summer and autumn several expeditions were sent out which deserve mention. One was to visit the Indian sachem, Massasoit, "their new freind," in order that they might

bestow upon him some gratuitie to bind him yͤ faster unto them; as also that hearby they might veiw yͤ countrie, and see in what maner he lived, what strength he had aboute him, and how yͤ ways were to his place.

So, on July 12, they sent off Edward Winslow and Stephen Hopkins, with Squanto to guide them, carrying as gifts "a suite of cloaths, and a horsemans coate, with some other small things." They were not much impressed with what they saw. The plague had decimated his people a few years before, as has been related, so that but few remained, and these were destitute and dirty. The journey of the envoys was tedious and apparently they did not follow the shortest possible route. Probably, however, it was then the easiest and therefore practically the shortest. It took them some forty miles westward from Plymouth, through the present Middleborough and Taunton to Swansea on Narragansett Bay and back. "They found but short comons, and came both weary & hungrie home," is Bradford's terse comment on the trip.

A second expedition was sent towards the end of July to Nauset on Cape Cod after John Billington, one of the boys in almost the only habitually restless and troublesome family in the colony,[3] who had lost himself in the woods and fallen among the Indians. The Pilgrims heard

The First Year.

of his whereabouts through Massasoit and sent their shallop after him and brought him back. In the fact that Bradford says that they "had him delivered" and that "those people also came and made their peace," there is no intimation that he had been detained among the Indians against his will, but only that he had fallen into the hands of a tribe which up to that time had had no intercourse with the settlers and which now exchanged gifts with them.

It is worth noting that the Pilgrims took advantage of this opportunity to find the owners of the corn which they had dug up in that vicinity in the previous November and to pay for it. About the middle of August they also were obliged to make a show of force toward some of the usually peaceable natives. Corbitant, an Indian ally of Massasoit but unfriendly to the English, was reported to have killed Squanto and another friendly Indian, Hobomok, some dozen miles west from Plymouth. The latter escaped and warned the colony but Squanto was detained. So the Pilgrims sent out Captain Standish and fourteen men, well armed, who wounded several of Corbitant's people slightly, before learning that Squanto was unharmed, and thereby taught the Indians a useful lesson or two and fortunately were not obliged to take life.

On Tuesday, September 28, they sent their first party northwards to Massachusetts Bay. It contained ten of their own men, besides Squanto and two other Indians, and went in the shallop. It was gone until Saturday, October 2. It appears to have landed first at the present Squantum, in Quincy, and to have crossed the bay later to where Charlestown now stands. It formed friendly relations with the Indians on each side of the bay and obtained a number of skins. It also was learned that the natives in that region were much afraid of the Tarratines, a tribe living in what is now Maine but often invading Massachusetts. It has been asserted so frequently that the Pilgrims abused the Indians[4] that it is proper to add here a quotation from Edward Winslow's published account of the trip, which sets forth the policy which they pursued habitually.

> Here Tisquantum [Squanto] would haue had vs rifled the Saluage women, and taken their skins, and all such things as might be seruiceable for vs; for (sayd he) they are a bad people, and haue oft threatned you: But our answere was; Were they neuer so bad, we would not wrong them, or giue them any just occasion against vs. for their words we little weighed them, but if they once attempted any thing against vs then we would deale far worse then he desired.

The explorers liked Massachusetts Bay so well as to wish that the colony had been established there.

CHAPTER XIX.

MORE HAPS AND MISHAPS.

AUTUMN had now come, and the work of gathering their harvest and making ready for the winter demanded attention. Whether the previous winter had been uncommonly severe or not, they could not be certain that the coming cold season would not prove equally trying. So they took all possible means to prepare for the worst. Their crop of corn was small, but at first it appeared to be sufficient, and they sought to supplement it with a store of fish and game. Says Bradford : —

They begane now to gather in ye small harvest they had, and to fitte up their houses and dwellings against winter, being all well recovered in health & strenght, and had all things in good plenty; for as some were thus imployed in affairs abroad, others were excersised in fishing, aboute cod, & bass, &

other fish, of which y^ey tooke good store, of which every family had their portion. All ye som̄er ther was no wante. And now begane to come in store of foule, as winter approached, of which this place did abound when they came first (but afterward decreased by degrees). And besids water foule, ther was great store of wild Turkies, of which they tooke many, besids venison, &c. Besids they had aboute a peck a meale a weeke to a person, or now since harvest, Indean corne to y^t proportion. Which made many afterwards write so largly of their plenty hear to their freinds in England, which were not fained, but true reports.[1]

This confidence in the sufficiency of their supplies, however, was soon destroyed. On November 21 the Fortune arrived, a small ship sent by the London Company, which had been on the way since early in July, in which came thirty-five additional settlers, together with Robert Cushman, who had started with the Pilgrims on their own voyage and had returned in the Speedwell.

Partly because of imperfect original equipment and partly because of the excessive length of the voyage, the Fortune's company arrived in a state of lamentable want. Probably the colonists had received no announcement of her coming until they discovered her heading into Plymouth Bay; but then, after assuring themselves that she was not hostile, they must have assumed with rejoicing that she had come laden with the various supplies of which it was well known at home that they would be in need. But any such assumption had to be abandoned as soon as she had dropped anchor. Instead of adding anything of value to the resources of the colony, her company had to be fed and cared for, and the colonists even had to furnish the ship some provisions in order that she might reach England again. Some suits of clothing seem to have been all which she brought as cargo which was of much use. So reduced were her people that there remained on board

> not so much as bisket-cake or any other victialls for them, neither had they any bediug, but some

More Haps and Mishaps. 225

sory things they had in their cabins, nor pot, nor pan, to drese any meate in; nor overmany cloaths, for many of them had brusht away their coats & cloaks at Plimoth [in England, where they had touched] as they came. . . . The plantation was glad of this addition of strenght, but could have wished that many of them had been of beter condition, and all of them beter furnished with provissions; but y^t could not be helpte.

It is plain that the Adventurers in England, who had engaged to see that the colony was properly supplied with what it needed, were shamefully negligent in respect to both quantity and quality of the goods sent out. It is evident, also, that little or no care was used to select proper persons as additional colonists. The Pilgrims had become so reduced in numbers that they would have been glad of more people if these had been suitably equipped, but more mouths without more food only embarrassed them. With their accustomed courage, however, they made the best of the situation. But they had to bear an additional annoyance and of a peculiarly painful sort. Mr. Cushman, who had not come to remain, brought letters from Thomas Weston and his associates reproaching the Pilgrims for not having sent back a cargo in the Mayflower. In view of their knowledge of the sufferings of the colony during the Mayflower's delay there, the unfairness of these letters is remarkable and betrays the sordid greed of most of the Adventurers and their almost complete indifference to the needs of the colonists.

It would have been only natural for them to be disappointed by the delay of profits from their investments in the colonial undertaking, had the circumstances rendered such returns possible, but they ought to have understood that their own failure to equip the Pilgrims properly at first, and to send out to them sufficient supplies until the colony had become established and prosperous, was the true cause of this delay. Cushman, however, managed to induce the Pilgrims to sign the contract with the Adventurers which they had refused to sign at Southampton. Doubtless they felt that almost any material concession was better than to risk losing wholly the evidently declining interest of the London merchants. The Fortune made only a short stay. She sailed for home at the end of a fortnight, Cushman returning in her, and she carried back about £500 worth of clapboards, skins, and other goods which had been accumulated for this purpose. Governor Bradford also sent by her a manly letter defending himself and his companions from Weston's accusations.

Then precautions against famine had to be taken at once.

The Gove^r & his assistante haveing disposed these late comers into severall families, as y^{ey} best could, tooke an exacte accounte of all their provisions in store, and proportioned ye same to ye number of persons, and found that it would not hould out above 6. months at halfe alowance, and hardly that. And they could not well give less this winter time till fish came in againe. So they were presently put to half alowance, one as well as an other, which begane to be hard, but they bore it patiently under hope of supply.

This decided manner of dealing with the situation was of course inevitable, but it must have been doubly unpleasant in view of the previous general understanding that the supply of provisions was sufficient. But at the time when they had supposed themselves to have food enough to last through the winter they had numbered only some fifty persons. The addition of thirty-five more was a serious matter. Many of these new-comers also were "lusty yonge men," sure to be among the hungriest and not likely to be especially patient or considerate, for they had come to the colony recklessly rather than with serious purpose and sympathy with its object. Bradford describes them as being "many of them wild enough, who litle considered whither or aboute what they wente, till they came into ye harbore at Cap Codd, and ther saw nothing but a naked and barren place." Plainly they were more of a hindrance than a help to the colony.

Three incidents which befell during this same year deserve mention here. One, which occurred on June 28, is the first recorded attempt at a duel in New England if not in America.[2] Although the Pilgrims were ready enough to fight in self-defence against any common foe, they were far from approving of private combats. But one was undertaken in their midst. Edward Doten and Edward Leister, the two servants of Stephen Hopkins, had a quarrel and foolishly determined to settle it with swords and daggers. One was wounded in the hand and the other in the thigh. They were promptly arrested and were tried with solemn formality before the whole company. They were condemned to be tied together by the hands and feet and left without food or drink for twenty-four hours. But, after having endured this uncomfortable, ignominious, and suitably ridiculous penalty for only one hour, they pleaded so hard for relief and promised good behavior so earnestly that, upon Mr. Hopkins's intercession, they were released. Their experience appears to have checked any tendency towards duelling in the colony completely.

The second was more serious. Soon after the Fortune had sailed, at about the end of November, a new alarm was caused by the Indians. The largest and most warlike tribe near enough to Plymouth to take much notice of the colony was the Narragansett, which occupied most of what now is the State of Rhode Island. It is stated to have numbered 30,000, of whom 5,000 were warriors.[3] Perhaps this tribe had learned of the reduced numbers of the colony, which hardly can have been kept secret permanently. At any rate it undertook to intimidate the colonists and sent a messenger to Plymouth with a bundl of arrows tyed aboute with a great sneak-skine [snake-skin]; which their interpretours tould them [that is, the settlers] was a threatening & a chaleng.

But the Indians had misunderstood the spirit of the Pilgrims.

Y^e Govr, with ye advice of others, sente them a round answere, that if they had rather have warre then peace, they might begine when they would; they had done them no wrong, neither did y^{ey} fear them, or should they find them unprovided. And by another messenger sente ye sneake-skine back with bullits in it; but they would not receive it, but sent it back againe.

This reply quenched the ardor of the Narragansetts for war, but the Pilgrims at once set at work to renew and improve their military organization, and built a fence, with gates and "flankers," [4] all around the settlement, and maintained a systematic watch at night and sometimes by day.

The third incident occurred on Christmas. Says Bradford: —

I shall remmember one passage more, rather of mirth then of waight. One ye day called Christmas-day, ye Govr caled them out to worke, (as was used,) but ye most of this new-company [the thirty-five] excused them selves and said it wente against their consciences to work on y^t day. So ye Govr tould them that if they made it mater of conscience, he would spare them till they were better informed. So he led-away ye rest and left them; but when they came home at noone from their worke, he found them in ye streete at play, openly; some pitching ye barr, & some at stoole-ball, and shuch like sports. So he went to them, and tooke away their implements, and tould them that was against his conscience, that they should play & others worke. If they made ye keeping of it mater of devotion, let them kepe their houses, but ther should be no gameing or revelling in ye streets. Since which time nothing hath been atempted that way, at least openly.

Should this exercise of authority by the governor seem arbitrary to any reader, the fact ought to be recalled that the colony was face to face with threatening famine and already had been for some weeks on half allowance of food. Whatever the

governor's ideas about Christmas ordinarily may have been, in the existing circumstances he hardly could be blamed for objecting to untimely merrymakings. There was need, for the sake of the common safety, that every man should work his hardest and every day, and the release of the young men from toil for that occasion was a generous concession, especially in view of the probable insincerity of their plea of conscience.

CHAPTER XX.

TREMBLING IN THE BALANCE.

THE depressing uncertainty in regard to the life of the colony continued for several years. It proved to be almost impossible to establish themselves successfully and it is surprising that the attempt was not abandoned. As already has been explained, most of the members of the London company, the Adventurers, were so ignorant of or indifferent to the needs of the colony, besides being very jealous and quarrelsome mutually, that it did little to contribute to the prosperity of the Pilgrims or even to secure them a bare sustenance. Out of the six or seven vessels which made harbor at Plymouth during 1622 and 1623 only the last two appear to have been sent by the Adventurers. In May, 1622, a shallop reached Plymouth from the Sparrow, a ship which Weston had sent fishing to the Maine coast, in which were brought seven passengers and some letters.[1] About the end of June the Charity touched there, on her way for Weston to Virginia, but brought them no goods or provisions; and the colony had to help feed her people, about sixty, during her stay, and keep and care for a number of them who were ill during "ye most parte of ye somer," until she came in again on her way home.[2]

In the autumn the Discovery, owned by English merchants not among the Adventurers, touched at the colony, and the Pilgrims were able to procure from her some beads and knives for trade with the Indians, but at exorbitant prices, and they obtained from her no food.[3] Not long after, in the spring of 1623, another ship[4] reached them, sent out for himself by John Peirce, one of the Adventurers, who seems to have accompanied her, but there is no account of any addition to the supplies of the colony from this source. At about the last of June, Captain Francis West, commissioned as admiral of New England, arrived in the ship Plantation, but he, too, was only a visitor. They tried to buy food or seed from the master of this ship, who

had some 2. hh of pease to sell, but seeing their wants, held them at £9. sterling a hoggshead, & under £8. he would not take, and yet would have beaver at an under rate. But they tould him they had lived so long with out, and would doe still, rather then give so unreasonably.[5]

Apparently some individuals bought a small quantity of the peas, but the greed of the master prevented the sale of most of his stock. In July the Anne arrived, and early in August "ye pinass," the Little James, the two vessels bringing about sixty new colonists, among them George Morton and family, and some supplies, although not enough to support even the new-comers.[6] The old difficulty continued to exist. "All [that is, all the provision] ye company sent at any time was allways too short for those people yt came with it." [7] In their penury it must have been an inexpressible distress to the Pilgrims, who were bravely and loyally keeping their faith with the Adventurers, to hear from the mother country so seldom, and to have ship after ship arrive bringing no aid but usually in actual need of help from them. Yet they never failed to do all in their power for those who thus claimed their assistance.

Although their trials during the first winter had been of the severest character, they now were obliged to brave a new peril quite equal to any which had preceded it. The lack of food increased until they found themselves face to face with actual starvation, and the extremity of their want deserves to be set forth more at length. As early as May, 1622, "in a maner their provissions were wholy spent, and they looked hard for supply, but none came." [8] Not long after, however, they heard of a fishing-vessel somewhere off the northern coast, and Edward Winslow was sent to obtain provisions from her if possible. Fortunately he did not have to return quite empty-handed, yet he was able to procure but very little food in comparison with what they needed.

   He gott some good quantitie and returned in saftie. . . . But what was gott . . . being devided among so many, came to but a litle, yet by God's blesing it upheld them till harvest. It arose but to a quarter of a pound of bread a day to each person; and y[e] Gov[r] caused it to be dayly given them, otherwise, had it been in their owne custody, they would have eate it up & then starved. But thus, with what els they could get, they made pretie shift till corne was ripe.[9]

But the harvest time brought little and only temporary improvement. The conditions of the season may not have been sufficiently favorable, and in any case they cannot yet have become expert in raising corn. Indeed, Bradford declares this plainly. Moreover, the longer the scarcity of food continued the less able to perform physical labor they became.

All had their hungrie bellies filled. But it arose but to a litle, in comparison of a full year's supplie; partly by reason they were not yet well aquainted with ye maner of Indean corne, (and they had no other,) allso their many other imployments, but cheefly their weaknes for wante of food, to tend it as they should have done. Also much was stolne both by night & day, before it became scarce eatable, & much more afterward. And though many were well whipt (when they were taken) for a few ears of corne, yet hunger made others (whom conscience did not restraine) to venture.[10]

These thefts undoubtedly were committed chiefly, if not wholly, by persons who but recently had arrived in the colony. Fishing of course was pursued as much as possible, but its success was limited by their lack of sufficient equipment, and it was hard work and often unrewarding.

Haveing but one boat left . . . they were devided into severall companies, 6. or 7. to a gangg or company, and so wente out with a nett they had bought, to take bass & such like fish, by course. every company knowing their turne. No sooner was ye boate discharged of what she brought, but ye next company tooke her and wente out with her. Neither did they returne till they had cauight something, though it were 5. or 6. days before, for they knew ther was nothing at home, and to goe home emptie would be a great discouragemente to ye rest. . . . If she stayed longe or got litle, then all went to seeking of shelfish, which at low-water they digged out of ye sands. And this was their living in ye somer time, till God sente y^m beter; & in winter they were helped with ground-nuts and foule. Also in ye somer they gott now & then a dear.[11]

It is difficult to read this artless and pathetic record without profound emotion. What gallant courage, what loyalty to their beliefs, what intense faith in God the Pilgrims must have possessed in order to endure, after so many and so diversified previous trials, such distresses as these!

This discouraging and weakening condition of comparative famine continued about a year and a half, until the autumn of 1623. In the spring of that year they became convinced that something was amiss with their methods, and renewed study of the situation led them to alter their policy of labor in an important respect, which in view of modern discussions of the same subject should be described. Apparently there had prevailed among them to some extent a belief in what may be termed Christian Communism. It has been noted already that, when about to depart from Leyden,

those that weare to goe, prepared them selves with all speed, and sould of their estats and (such as were able) put in their moneys into ye commone stock, which was disposed by those appointed, for ye making of generall provissions.[12]

Apparently also after landing at Plymouth they practiced a modified communism, especially in regard to labor and its fruits. They had their individual houses but raised their crops in common and for general consumption. Each man worked four of the six days of the secular week for the public benefit, including that of the Adventurers in London as well as that of the colony itself, and only two days in his own interest. But when it had become clear that they must grow larger harvests or starve,

> after much debate of things, the Govr (with ye advise of ye cheefest amongest them) gave way that they should set corne every man for his owne perticuler, and in that regard trust to them selves; in all other things to goe on in ye generall way as before. . . . This had very good success; for it made all hands very industrious, so as much more corne was planted then other waise would have bene by any means ye Govr or any other could use.[13]

Bradford emphasizes the good results of this change of method and then adds:—

> The experience that was had in this comone course and condition, tried sundrie years, and that amongst godly and sober men, may well evince the vanitie of that conceit of Platos and other ancients, applauded by some of later times; — that ye taking away of propertie, and bringing in comunitie into a comone wealth, would make them happy and flourishing; as if they were wiser then God. For this comunitie (so farr as it was) was found to breed

much confusion & discontent, and retard much imploymēt that would have been to their benefite and comforte. . . . Upon ye poynte all being to have alike, and all to doe alike, they thought them selves in ye like condition, and one as good as another; and so, if it did not cut of those relations that God hath set amongest men, yet it did at least much diminish and take of ye mutuall respects that should be preserved amongst them. And would have been worse if they had been men of another condition.[14]

This is practical testimony and based upon experience and observation. It is worth being weighed carefully by those who theorize, as some do nowadays, about the establishment of socialistic or communistic settlements, in which most of the labor is to be performed for the general benefit. No such modern colony, it is safe to say, would be likely to be composed of more orderly, intelligent, diligent, or public-spirited settlers than those of the Plymouth Colony, and the policy of common labor as opposed to individual apparently had a fair trial among the Pilgrims and ought to have succeeded there if it can be depended upon to succeed in the long run anywhere. But it failed completely, and it is not likely that social conditions have altered sufficiently to render a different result probable now. Human nature varies little from age to age.

CHAPTER XXI.

THE DAWN OF BETTER DAYS.

THAT the longest night has an end is a true proverb, and by degrees the situation of the colony began to improve. Their change of policy about planting produced large crops in 1623 and afterwards they suffered less from scanty food, although one more alarm first disturbed their peace and even threatened their safety. Their hopes of this harvest were nearly shattered by a prolonged drought.

Notwithstand all their great paines & industrie, & ye great hops of a large cropp, the Lord seemed to blast, & take away the same, and to threaten further & more sore famine unto them, by a great drought which continued from ye 3. weeke in May, till about ye midle of July, without any raine, and with great heat (for ye most parte), insomuch as ye corne begane to wither away . . . and some of ye drier grounds were partched like withered hay.[1]

After having done all in their own power to remedy the situation in vain, they had recourse to the Almighty, and their prayers were followed by the rain.

> They sett a parte a solemne day of humilliation, to seeke ye Lord by humble & fervente prayer, in this great distrese. And he was pleased to give them a gracious & speedy answer, both to their owne, and the Indeans admiration, that lived amongest them. For all ye morning, and greatest part of the day, it was clear weather & very hotte, and not a cloud or any signe of raine to be seen, yet toward evening it begane to overcast, and shortly after to raine, with shuch sweete and gentle showers, as gave them cause of rejoyceing, & blessing God. . . . Which did so apparently revive & quicken ye decayed corne & other fruits, as was wonderfull to see, and made ye Indeans astonished to behold; and afterwards the Lord sent them shuch seasonable showers, with enterchange of faire warme weather, as, through his blessing, caused a fruitfull & liberall harvest.

Moreover, they had become accustomed to the climate of their new home. The surviving original settlers gradually had established themselves in a condition of

The Blockhouse.

moderate comfort, and such new-comers as had joined the colony had been spared the pain and risk of undergoing many of its early hardships. The general health, therefore, was much improved and the death rate fell to something like its normal figures.

They also had little more trouble from the Indians. In the spring of 1622 they heard that the Narragansetts were about to attack them, but it proved a false alarm, although it caused a temporary and probably unfounded suspicion that Squanto was insincere.[2] But some rivalry, not to say jealousy, between him, Massasoit, and Hobomok, enabled the Pilgrims to manage them all safely, and in the autumn Squanto died,

desiring ye Govr to pray for him, that he might goe to ye Englishmens God in heaven, and bequeathed sundrie of his things to sundry of his English freinds, as remembrances of his love; of whom they had a great loss.[3]

He had been of inestimable service to

them and there seems little reason to doubt his loyalty. Early in the next year, 1623, they cured Massasoit of a serious illness and in gratitude he revealed to them the fact of an extensive Indian conspiracy against them.[4] This was the most dangerous as, indeed, it proved to be the only serious peril in their whole experience with the Indians. With their usual energy they determined to strike the first blow, having ample proof of their danger; and on April 4 Standish and eight others with Hobomok set sail for Wessagusset, where on April 6 they attacked the hostile Indians, killed the two chiefs, Pecksuot and Wituwamat, and five others, who were about to attack them, and frightened all the neighboring tribes exceedingly.[5]

In the summer of this same year they built on what is called Burial Hill, which rises one hundred and sixty-five feet above the sea level, a fort

both strong & comly, which was of good defence, made with a flate rofe & battlments, on which their ordnance were mounted, and wher they kepte constante watch, espetially in time of danger. It served them allso for a meeting house, and was fitted accordingly for that use.[6]

The ordnance, says Isaac De Rasieres, the diplomatic agent of the Dutch in the New Netherlands, who visited Plymouth in 1627, consisted of "six cannons, which shoot iron balls of four or five pounds and command the surrounding country." The same witness describes picturesquely their manner of going to church, as follows : —

They assemble by beat of drum, each with his musket or firelock, in front of the captain's door; they have their cloaks on, and place themselves in order, three abreast, and are led by a sergeant without beat of drum. Behind comes the Governor, in a long robe; beside him on the right hand comes the preacher with his cloak on, and on the left hand the captain with his side-arms and cloak on, and with a small cane in his hand; and so they march in good order, and each sets his arms down near him.[7]

The colony had no regular minister for about nine years, and during this interval

William Brewster, although he never administered the sacraments, "taught twise every Saboth, and yt both powerfully and profitably, to ye great contentment of ye hearers, and their comfortable edification; yea, many were brought to God by his ministrie."[8] Doubtless he was "the preacher" to whom De Rasieres referred.[9]

It has been mentioned that the Anne and the Little James, which arrived in the summer of 1623, brought a considerable addition to the colony, not less than sixty persons.[10] Most of them were "very usefull" and "became good members to ye body," and some were the wives and children of original settlers. Others, however, were so bad that they had to be sent home the next year. A number of them, also, had come "on their perticuler," which seems to mean that they were an organized company willing to submit to the laws of the colony yet desirous of maintaining their own organization.[11] The Pilgrims readily arranged satisfactory mutual relations with them, and most of them became useful citizens and were absorbed in due time and naturally in the general colony. Yet the food question still was so serious when these new colonists came that it was determined finally that they should subsist upon the provisions which they had brought, the earlier settlers also depending upon their own, until the next year.[12] But the harvest gathered soon after set all fears at rest. "In stead of famine, now God gave them plentie, and ye face of things was changed . . . so as any generall wante or famine hath not been amongst them since."

In addition to the comfort of plenty, the Pilgrims also must have found cheer in the fact that they were able to hold their ground. In the spring of 1622 they learned that a general massacre by the Indians had occurred "in ye south-collonie of Virginia," in which nearly or quite three hundred and fifty English had perished.[13] At about the same time the nearest effort to found a new colony proved a total failure. The restless Thomas Weston, not even yet comprehending the hindrances to the carrying out of such an enterprise, had obtained a grant of land further north and sent a small colony to settle at Wessagusset, now Weymouth.[14] They visited Plymouth first and of course were equipped insufficiently, and the Pilgrims out of common humanity had to care for them a long time and just when it was hardest to take care of themselves, and after settling at Wessagusset their provisions soon ran out. They ill-treated the Indians and naturally had trouble, and the Pilgrims had to send a party under Standish to rescue them and enable them to abandon their settlement and get off to join the fishing fleet at the northward. The enterprise was bungled from the beginning and deserved its fate.

Early in 1623 Weston himself also appeared, but in sore need.[15] He had come over, in disguise for some reason, to visit his colony, which already had collapsed. He had been shipwrecked and in addition had been robbed by the Indians, and he barely reached Plymouth alive. The Pilgrims took pity upon him, too, and fitted him out afresh, so that he was able to make his way back to the northern fishing fleet, but he afterwards proved more unfriendly to them than ever. He must have been as ungrateful as he was reckless.

In September, 1623, a more considerable attempt was made to colonize in the same region. Captain Robert Gorges, who was commissioned to be "generall Gover of ye cuntrie," endeavored with a number of families and individuals to settle at Wessagusset, which Weston's colony had abandoned. He had large authority on paper, and the governor of the Plymouth Colony had been appointed one of his three Assistants. Weston reappeared about this time and Gorges called him to account for misconduct. A long controversy ensued, with which the Plymouth men managed to avoid being complicated annoyingly. Weston was arrested once or twice but released, and in a few months the colony of Gorges scattered and Gorges himself returned to England, "not finding the state of things hear to answer his quallitie and condition."[16] He was more desirous of exercising authority and of making a show than of engaging in hard work.

In connection with his undertaking occurred the first attempt of the spiritual authorities of England to regain control over the Pilgrims. He had brought over two clergymen of the Church of England. One was Rev. William Morell,[17] who remained about a year, apparently a part of the time at Plymouth, and who had been sent out to exercise some sort of ecclesiastical authority in New England. But he made no attempt in that direction, probably because there was no church except that in Plymouth, where small notice would have been taken of his claims; and he spent his time in composing a fairly meritorious Latin poem about New England, of which he made an English translation, and which, with the translation, he published after returning to England. The other was William Blackstone,[18] who soon became the pioneer settler of what is now the city of Boston. There is some dispute, however, whether he were not a Puritan, and he made no more effort to secure ecclesiastical recognition than Morell made. Apparently this outreaching of the Church of England authorities into the western world did not alarm the Pilgrims much.

During the same year other attempts were made to settle at Piscataqua, Monhegan, and elsewhere, in the hope of increasing the products of the fisheries by providing storehouses and caretakers so that fishing could be carried on during the larger part of the year, but all in vain.[19]

For some years the Pilgrims were the only colonists who had courage enough to face the inevitable hardships. Probably, had their own undertaking been merely commercial, they too would have abandoned it. But their religious liberty was at stake and their faith in God upheld them.

CHAPTER XXII.

THE COMMERCIAL HISTORY OF THE COLONY.

IT is worth while to consider somewhat more connectedly the history of the Plymouth Colony on its business side, even at the cost of some repetition of statements already made. First a few preliminary facts deserve notice. The Virginia Company had been formed in England in 1606 in order to establish trade with North America. In fact there were two companies, also called colonies, the First or Southern, which was to colonize the territory between the thirty-fourth and forty-first degrees of north latitude, and the Second or Northern, which was allotted the territory between the thirty-eighth and forty-fifth degrees, their grants overlapping. The grants of the two colonies were established by two patents[1], issued by King James on April 10, 1606. Each company was to be governed by a council of thirteen members. The first or London Company was that with which the Pilgrims had their earlier dealings, and it soon appropriated exclusively the title of the Virginia Company, the other often being called the Plymouth Company, named from Plymouth in England. The council of the former was divided by factions when negotiations with the Pilgrims were begun, but after some delays it granted a patent intended to cover the case of the Pilgrims, to a Mr. John Wincob.[2] He intended to accompany them but did not, nor was any use ever made of this patent, no copy of which is known to exist and the provisions of which also are unknown. What has been said thus far, it will be observed, relates merely to the possible location of the Pilgrim Colony.

We come now to the organization with which the Pilgrims stood in the relation of business partners. In 1619 or early in 1620 another commercial company had been formed of some seventy persons, chiefly living in or near London, called the Merchant Adventurers.[3] It was not a regular corporation but a kind of partnership, and although it professed to have a partly religious aim it was chiefly if not wholly intent on pecuniary gain. This company, among the managers of which Thomas Weston was prominent, undertook to back the Pilgrims financially, to aid in equipping them, and to furnish them with supplies until they could support themselves. A contract was drawn up of which the principal features were the provisions that the mutual relation should continue seven years, that until the end of that period all profits should be held in common, and that then all the houses, lands, and goods of the colony, and all other profits should be divided, the Adventurers taking half and the colonists half.

The modifications of these terms which the Pilgrims proposed, although they were not granted, certainly seem reasonable, but probably it was partly on their account, although the colonists finally yielded to Cushman's pleading in 1621 and signed the contract after all, and partly because of the previous disputes among the Adventurers that some of these withdrew wholly and others contributed reluctantly and scantily, so that interest in the undertaking largely died out and the Pilgrims were neglected grossly. It has been mentioned earlier that they actually had to sell some of their provisions in order to sail for America free of debt. Of course the success of the colony depended upon a sufficient, not to say a liberal, equipment, and if ordinary men and women had formed the Pilgrim band it would have been doomed before it started.

As has been said, they had obtained a patent from the Virginia or Southern Company, of which no use was made.

Apparently, rather than delay longer, they set out intending to take advantage of this patent if it continued good. They did not then mean to settle near Cape Cod but much farther west and south. But only a little while before they had started the Second, the Northern Company had sent a petition to the king for a new act of incorporation, as to which favorable although not final action had been taken. This was granted on November 13, 1620. It applied the name of New England for the first time to the territory concerned, included the country between the fortieth and forty-eighth parallels of latitude, and became the basis of subsequent patents.[4] It covered the actual location of the Pilgrim Colony. Doubtless the Pilgrims were aware of this petition and knew that after their change of plan and their decision to settle in Massachusetts their own patent after all might have no force. This may have been one reason why they drew up their compact. Circumstances having perhaps cut them off from the government under which they had meant to settle, they saw that they must provide, at least temporarily, some substitute of their own. On June 11, 1621, however, a new charter for their benefit was granted to "John Peirce and his associates," who were among the Adventurers, by "the President and Council of New England," apparently the managers of the Northern Company, within whose jurisdiction the colonists had settled.[5] Nearly a year later Peirce, who does not seem to have been much more honorable than Weston, secretly obtained a much more inclusive charter in his own name, but he finally was persuaded to turn it over to the company of Adventurers. Little is known of it except that Peirce brought several lawsuits on account of it against others, apparently in vain.[6]

The letter which announced the new charter, the first granted to Peirce, — the original copy of which, by the way, is now treasured at Plymouth, — reached them in the Fortune on November 21, 1621,[7] but the announcement seems to have made no particular difference to them. Weston wrote it and it was the same in which he reproached them bitterly for not having sent home a cargo in the Mayflower. During the next three or four years several ships were sent to the colony at long intervals, and a few others touched there on their way to Virginia or elsewhere. The colonists loaded the Fortune with skins and clapboards, but she was captured and plundered by the French, and they made what shift they could to find cargoes for subsequent vessels but with no great success for some time. Early in 1622 disagreements among the Adventurers became so sharp that Weston wrote to the colony proposing that the mutual contract be abandoned.[8] Governor Bradford prudently kept this news secret for a time, fearing that the courage of his associates would fail wholly if they should learn that the

Adventurers wished to abandon them, small although the aid received from that source had been; and his discretion was justified by a subsequent letter from Edward Pickering and William Greene, two other Adventurers, stating that their company had bought out Weston, who had been seeking to deceive the Pilgrims and meant to injure them.[9] He soon proceeded to send out ships and set up his rival colony at Wessagusset, the speedy collapse of which already has been mentioned.

In 1623 Edward Winslow was sent back to England in the Anne to confer with the Adventurers and procure supplies for the colony, and in 1625 he returned with clothing, a few cattle, and other necessaries, but reported a strong hostile faction in the London Company and a great reluctance to allow the remainder of the Pilgrims, who had been left in Leyden, to join the Plymouth people.[10] Meanwhile, the Adventurers had sent over the "pinass," the Little James, to be kept by the colony and used as a fishing and cruising ship. But she soon was wrecked and sunk and after being raised was sent back. The next year, 1625, she came over again, but was captured by the Turks on her return voyage, with her load of fish and furs. Another and larger ship in company with her carried home a full cargo, but rumors of war between England and France caused her to put into one or two English ports instead of making straight for Bilbao, her destination, and the delay cost her her market. In 1624 the colony, through Winslow and Robert Cushman, the former being in England where the latter had remained, obtained a patent covering land for a fishing station at Cape Ann, but no permanent use was made of it.[11] In this same year an excellent ship-carpenter, whose services they greatly needed, was sent over to Plymouth, but he soon died, and another man, sent out to make salt for them, proved wholly incompetent. Prosperity did not come to them speedily even after their fortunes had begun to improve.

In 1624 their difficulties with John Lyford and John Oldham began, which resulted in breaking up the company of the Adventurers and in securing for the colony a new agreement, by which their commercial independence finally was attained. The former had just arrived. The latter had come in the Anne. Lyford was a reprobate but nominally a clergyman of the Church of England. Avowing a wish to join the church in Plymouth, he was received and treated with great respect. But he and Oldham soon were detected in a conspiracy against the public welfare. They were tried and convicted. The particulars need not be narrated. Lyford professed deep penitence and was pardoned. But he soon turned out to be both treacherous and corrupt and finally was expelled from Plymouth. He went to Nantasket and then to Salem and died at last in Virginia. Oldham also was expelled from the colony, and more speedily. In 1625 Oldham reappeared, more violent than ever, but they dealt with him summarily. They

> apointed a gard of musketers wch he was to pass throw, and ever one was ordered to give him a thump . . . with ye but end of his musket, and then [he] was conveied to ye water side, wher a boat was ready to cary him away. Then they bid him goe & mende his maners.[12]

Not long after he repented and the Plymouth men good-naturedly became reconciled to him and had no further annoyance from him. He settled at Nantasket, went back to England, and was active in planning with the Gorges family for the settlement of the Bay, returned to America after the Bay colony had been established by others, and lived afterwards at Watertown, and in 1636 was killed by Indians. These men had friends among the London Adventurers, and a dispute over them finally broke up that company.[13]

It had been rent by divisions from the first, had suffered heavy losses and there was no prospect of greater harmony and success. But the Pilgrims had no desire to take advantage of this condition of affairs, and finally, through Standish and Allerton, who successively had been sent to England on the business, they agreed to pay £1,800 within six years, thereby purchasing their financial freedom.[14] Allerton paid £200 down and brought back £400 worth of supplies. The colony was reorganized at once for better farming and trade, and, in spite of their burden of debt, they entered courageously upon their new and at last independent career. This arrangement was accomplished in 1627 and 1628.

They never possessed a royal charter. But in 1629 the Council of New England, of which the Earl of Warwick then was president, granted to the colony of New Plymouth a new patent, made out to " William Bradford, his heirs, associates and assigns."[15] It is dated January 23, 1630, and the original parchment is in the office of the Register of Deeds at Plymouth. It defines the territorial limits of the colony for the first time and it also includes a grant of land for fifteen miles on each side of the Kennebec River, which they obtained in order to establish a fishing and trading station there. They came near being wrecked financially after all, for in 1631 Allerton proved to have mismanaged their funds and to have incurred debts in their name to the large amount of £4,770, in addition to which they still owed £1,000 of their purchase money.[16] But good fortune smiled upon them and by great exertions they appear to have paid all their obligations in full in the course of 1633.[17]

CHAPTER XXIII.

SUCCEEDING YEARS.

BEFORE the scheme of buying out the share of the Adventurers in their common interest had been carried out, several incidents had occurred in the domestic life of the colony which deserve brief notice. On November 15, 1623, a fire was caused by the carelessness or malice of some sailors belonging to a ship lying in the harbor, who were "roystering" ashore. The thatch upon the roof of the building in which they were ignited, and that house, as well as several others, was destroyed with all the goods and provisions in them. The common house, which stood next door and was full of valuable stores, was barely saved. Of course the sailors insisted that the fire was accidental, but it probably was set, yet incendiarism could not be proved. The settlement had a narrow escape from ruin.[1] At the annual election in 1624 Governor Bradford desired to retire. The colony insisted upon reëlecting him, however, but chose five Assistants for his relief instead of one.[2]

Later seven Assistants became customary, and the governor had two votes. This simple, democratic government seems to be all which the colony had, or needed, for a considerable period. The officials cannot have had much to do beyond supplying the proper authority for the general control of the settlers, preserving good order, collecting and expending their small taxes after it had become necessary to levy any, managing their common business relations with the Adventurers, and occasionally acting as the representatives of the colony in its intercourse with the Indians or with other settlers at Massachusetts Bay or elsewhere. They did not even appoint a constable until 1633 and had no tithing-man until 1694, long after the union with the Bay Colony.[3] Trials were held before the whole body of freemen until the end of 1623, when, as Goodwin states, it was enacted on December 27 that "all criminal facts, and also all matters of trespasses and debts between man and man, should be tried by the verdict of twelve honest men, to be impanelled by authority, in form of a jury, upon their oath."[4]

In the same year some of those who still were "on their particuler," that is, laboring outside of, although by leave of, the organized body of colonists, created some disaffection among certain of the more impressionable members of the body, and the latter demanded to be released from their obligations. A faction among the Adventurers in England was strongly suspected, if not actually known, to be behind this movement. After deliberation it was agreed that they should continue to dwell in the colony until the original term of partnership with the Adventurers, seven years, should have expired; that they should support themselves during the interval; and, at its end, should recompense the colony for its charges on their behalf by paying into the common stock half of all property which they should have accumulated above their food. This arrangement was as shrewd as it was just. No reasonable objection could be offered to it, yet it prevented those who might accept it from gaining any great advantage by the change, and but a few finally took advantage of it.[5]

During the same year Bradford and Brewster each received an affectionate letter from John Robinson, written in December, 1623, at Leyden.[6] In the former he lamented earnestly the killing of the seven Indians by the expedition under Captain Standish at Weymouth early in 1623, apparently a justifiable and even necessary use of force. Had Robinson understood the situation he would have regretted the necessity equally, but probably would not have protested as he did. His letter, however, was characteristically beautiful in spirit. In the spring of 1626 came another letter to Governor Bradford and Elder Brewster, written from Leyden by Roger White, which described touchingly the last illness and the death of Robinson, on March 1, 1625. Said Mr. White: —

> If either prayers, tears, or means, would have saved his life, he had not gone hence. But he having faithfully finished his course, and performed his worke which ye Lord had appointed him here to doe, he now resteth with ye Lord in eternall happines. We wanting him & all Church Gov^rs, yet we still (by ye mercie of God) continue & hould close togeather, in peace and quietnes; and so hope we shall doe, though we be very weake. Wishing (if such were ye will of God) that you & we were againe united togeather in one, either ther or here; but seeing it is ye will of ye Lord thus to dispose of things, we must labour wth patience to rest contented till it please ye Lord otherwise to dispose.[7]

This glimpse of the condition of those

who had remained in Leyden shows that prosperity there had been as difficult to be attained as had been feared.

In 1627 a kind of stock company was formed, in order to provide for the fulfillment of their new agreement with the Adventurers.[8] Each unmarried free man, that is, each unmarried man who was not a servant, was allotted one share, and each head of a family one for himself and one apiece for the other members of his family. Their cattle were distributed as nearly equally as possible, and the land lying near the town also was divided up at the rate of twenty acres to each share, the holders also retaining whatever land, apparently in single acres, they had owned previously. No meadow land for mowing was allotted,

but every season all were appoynted wher they should mowe, according to ye proportion of catle they had. . . . Also they gave ye Gover & 4. or 5. of ye spetiall men amongst them, ye houses they lived in; ye rest were valued & equalised at an indifferent rate, and so every man kept his owne, and he that had a better alowed some thing to him that had a worse, as ye valuation wente.

This arrangement "gave generally good contente, and setled men's minds." Each shareholder also was to assume his proportion of the common debts and of the purchase money pledged to the Adventurers. During the previous winter a ship bound for Virginia had been wrecked on the south side of Cape Cod, and the Pilgrims had to shelter her company, which was numerous, until the end of the next summer. They obtained from her various useful commodities, however.[9] During the same season, in order to enlarge their facilities for fishing and trading, they built a boat and a house and established a few men at Manomet in the present Sandwich, so as to have access, by portage of a few miles from one creek to another, into Buzzard's Bay, and thus avoid the dangers of Cape Cod,[10] and the measure proved quite profitable. At about this time also they received letters and messages in Dutch and French from the Dutch settlers at New Netherlands, now New York,[11] and for some years subsequently they had occasional communication and some trade with this western colony.

In 1628 they were compelled to exert their influence once more for good order beyond the bounds of their own territory. They had trouble with the famous, or infamous, Thomas Morton, of Merry Mount, who, by the way, was in no way related, so far as ever has become known, to his respectable namesakes, the Mortons of their own colony. In the spring of 1625 one Captain Wollaston, with a considerable company, among whom was a certain Thomas Morton, had attempted to settle in that part of the present Quincy which from him has come to be known as Mount Wollaston.[12] He soon had wearied of the undertaking and carried most of his companions away to Virginia. Morton, however, had remained with others. He ejected Wollaston's lieutenant, Fitcher, who had been left in charge, and entered upon a scandalous, dangerous career, even supplying the Indians with arms and ammunition, which the Plymouth men and others who now were trying to gain a foothold here and there in the country saw must be suppressed. The Plymouth colonists, therefore, first admonished him in friendly fashion, then warned him faithfully, and finally, he remaining obdurate, sent up Captain Standish with a party. They captured him and his followers and brought him to Plymouth, whence he soon was shipped off to England for the Council of New England to punish. But he escaped penalty somehow, and the next year Allerton foolishly brought him back to Plymouth as a sort of private secretary. He soon was sent away, returned to Mount Wollaston, resumed his evil courses, and after some seventeen years more of an equally checkered career, in the course of which he turned up again at Plymouth for a short time, where he was treated very coolly, he finally died in Maine. He wrote a book called *The New English Canaan*, which the sober settlers considered "infamous and scurrilous," but it contained some valuable information.

Meanwhile the region around and near Massachusetts Bay had slowly begun to be settled. The site of the present Salem had been occupied in 1626,[13] and John Endicott's company landed there on September 6, 1628.[14] Communication with this colony began soon and gradually became frequent. The difficulty about Thomas Morton was felt alike by the two colonies; the Plymouth men sent their physician, Dr. Samuel Fuller, to Salem when its people were suffering from scurvy, which kindness Endicott acknowledged in a grateful letter,[15] and in July, 1629, Deacon Charles Gott, of the Salem church, wrote to Plymouth announcing that a pastor and a teacher had been chosen, and that August 6 had been set apart for the election and ordination of elders and deacons, on which occasion Governor Bradford and others from Plymouth were present and expressed the fellowship of their own church.[16]

At about this time, too, the Pilgrims at last obtained a minister of the gospel. In 1628 Mr. Allerton had brought over to Plymouth a young man, by name Rogers, to serve the colony in this office; but they knew too little about him to accept him, and he proved crazy, so they sent him back.[17] But in 1629 Mr. Ralph Smith, who had been a minister, and whose sympathies were with the Separatists, came to Plymouth from the Bay Colony, and after becoming acquainted with him they approved him as their pastor.[18] Then for the first time since leaving Holland they became fully equipped ecclesiastically and once more enjoyed the sacraments. In the same year, or soon after, most of the Leyden remnant of the Pilgrim body came over to Plymouth in two companies,[19] apparently landing first at Salem and Charlestown. Thus the long and perilous emigration from England to America was consummated, and Holland knew the Pilgrims in the flesh no more.

CHAPTER XXIV.

EARLY LIFE IN THE COLONY.

THE life of the young colony seldom has been described, but such descriptions are worth being attempted although that now to be given must be based, as the others have been, upon inferences from a few known facts rather than upon full records. The Pilgrims had no newspapers, and not many journals written by individuals among them have come down to us. Nor do many of their letters remain. Probably they corresponded only seldom with their friends in the mother country, for opportunities of communication were rare. Indeed, theirs was not a letter-writing age like our own, and most of their letters at this time must have related principally to business affairs or religious and ecclesiastical topics. John

PLYMOUTH IN 1622.

storehouse; then in order come the houses of P. Brown, J. Goodman, Allerton, F. Cooke, E. Winslow. The house in the enclosure on the . The fort appears at the top of the hill.

Robinson's last letters, written from Leyden in December, 1623, to Governor Bradford and Elder Brewster,[1] although sent to the colony instead of from it, and the more than thirty contents of Governor Bradford's own Letter-Book,[2] written by various persons, probably are fair examples of the usual character of the correspondence of the period, at any rate among them, and contain very little of the personal or general information, except upon the classes of subjects just suggested, with which most modern letters abound.

The habits and manners of the Pilgrims were so simple and so similar in general to those of their friends at home that it hardly would have been natural for them to describe such things at length upon paper. Some significant statements occur in Governor Bradford's history and in accounts of their observations in the colony by a few such visitors as De Rasieres, already mentioned, but these are incomplete and far from numerous. It is possible, however, to form a reasonably satisfactory idea of colonial life from the scanty sources which exist. Let us try to picture it about the years 1622–23, for example.

The little village, still chiefly aligned along the opposite sides, and mostly upon the south side, of its short street, — which can have had no pavement nor any sidewalks, — was growing, but cannot yet have included at the most more than ten or a dozen[3] dwellings with a few outbuildings. Doubtless they were merely log houses, possessing but a single story, or at most one story and an attic, with their crevices plastered with clay[4] and with earth or turf banked up around their foundations for the sake of warmth. The roofs were thatched and most of the chimneys probably were constructed upon the outside. Within, as no sawmill had yet been built, the floors must have been made of planks roughly hewn out by the axe, and doubtless many consisted simply of hard-trodden earth. In either case they are likely to have been sprinkled thickly with frequently renewed sand or rushes. There may have been a few rugs or carpets in the colony, but they cannot have been numerous at this time.[5] Nor can they have possessed much window glass. Most of the windows, if they had in them anything else than wooden shutters, must have been filled with oiled paper[6] or some other imperfect substitute for glass. They must have used candles principally after dark, but they certainly had some lamps.[7]

Presumably most of the houses contained not more than three or four rooms apiece, furnished plainly and in many instances only coarsely, although in some of them chairs, tables, cradles, spinning-wheels, desks, clocks, chests, and other articles, brought from England or Holland and precious because of their associations, must have stood side by side with the ruder constructions which necessity had compelled them to shape for themselves.

Probably much of their tableware was wooden, yet in many households pewter spoons, platters, etc., were to be seen. Possibly also they owned a little silver. Matchlocks, powder-horns, bullet-pouches, and swords rather than pictures must have hung upon their walls, although perhaps they owned a few family portraits; and books cannot have abounded among them. Doubtless copies of the Bible were most common. The so-called King James version hardly can have become widely known by their time, and there is every probability that they used the Genevan version.[8] A few of the best educated or formerly most prosperous settlers possessed small libraries. It is known, for example, that Elder Brewster left at his death a well-selected and remarkably diversified collection, numbering about four hundred volumes, of which, judging by their dates of publication, he may have brought nearly three fourths over with him in the Mayflower.[9] Bradford left two hundred and seventy-five books, and Fuller and Standish are known to have had small collections.

The costumes customarily worn in the colony must in general have been such as then were usual in England, and they are familiar to many modern eyes through old portraits and other pictures. Those of the men seem to have been the more picturesque, and consisted of doublets or short coats, belted at the waist and commonly surmounted by wide linen collars. Similar cuffs often were worn at the wrists. They also wore knee breeches, long stockings, and stout shoes, sometimes with large buckles over the instep. Their hats probably were made of felt and had high, conical crowns and broad and often flapping brims. Loose cloaks also were common. The dress of the women, although not ungraceful, probably differed less from that of the simplest and plainest modern life and in general resembled it. All seem to have preferred dark or neutral colors and to have avoided much in the way of ornament, yet they were not without brightly colored garments.[10] Unless they were better provided at first with clothing than they were with other necessary supplies, many of them must have been in great need before prosperity enabled them to renew their stock, and some of them may have been reduced at times to the use of skins and other substitutes for cloth.

On the brow of a low hill affording a fine view of the bay, the historic Burial Hill, but known among them for some time as Fort Hill,[11] close at hand and commanding the village, stood the blockhouse, or fort, prepared to shelter and defend them in case of attack by any enemy and used also as their meeting-house on the Sabbath. Although apparently it was considerably larger than any one of their dwellings, it must have been constructed in much the same manner as these and cannot have been imposing in either size or architecture. Around and behind their homes lay their little gardens and beyond these the fields, which they gradually broke up and tilled. At first they were obliged to go only about an eighth of a mile to reach the surrounding woods, but their inroads upon the forest for fuel and building material must gradually have pushed back its nearest edge. No roads extended from the tiny settlement in any direction. A few footpaths through the underbrush, narrow, uneven, and winding, were their sole ways of egress except as it was possible to skirt the shore, where lay their only boat, to the north or south upon the sandy beach.

As yet their barns and fields were bare of cattle,[12] but by 1624 they had "many swine and poultry" and a number of goats.[13] Even household pets must have been very few, but mention is made of a "great Mastiffe" and a "little spannel," and probably they had a few cats.

Their lives must have been laborious to an extreme degree. Such pleasures as they were able to enjoy must have been almost wholly domestic or neighborly. They had no lectures, concerts, or other such entertainments. Apparently they observed no public holidays except an occasional Thanksgiving or Fast Day. In order to secure moderate comfort and even to maintain their existence they were obliged to devote almost their whole time, except upon the Sabbath, to energetic toil. Even the women and children went into the fields and helped with the corn planting at the time when threatening famine led to the distribution of the land into individual allotments. But ordinarily the women doubtless confined themselves to the customary domestic duties and the care of the sick, and were abundantly busy with these employments; the men constructed buildings, brought fuel, tilled the fields, and hunted the wild game of the forest or sought to catch the fish of the ocean or the neighboring brooks for food; and the children aided their parents in the house and the garden and studied or occasionally played like other children. It has been claimed by some that a common school was established almost as soon as the colony had been founded. But the earliest record of any such institution is in 1670.[14] It cannot be that such a company as the Pilgrims neglected education for fifty years, and the natural inference, which a few hints support, is that the children were taught in one or more private schools, which doubtless were as good as public schools then could have been. And at first for some years they seem to have been educated only at home.

After the provisions which they had brought over in the Mayflower had been exhausted, their food for several years consisted wholly of what they could raise or obtain otherwise for themselves. They had provided themselves with English wheat, peas, and some other kinds of seed for planting, but for some reason these crops failed entirely. Except for the

Indian corn which they found or bought of the natives and learned from Squanto how to cultivate, and from which they made the coarse but nourishing meal now familiar to all New Englanders, they must have starved. Too often they had much less even of that than they needed. After it became plentiful, however, they used it as money for a time. But they shot wild turkeys and smaller birds and now and then a deer in the woods and sea fowl along the shore, and they dug clams and mussels from the beach and caught cod, bass, and other fish, probably including alewives, in the water. Thus they ordinarily managed to obtain food enough, although, as has been narrated, there were times when these sources of supply almost failed and they were in dire distress. Fortunately, although there are indications that they missed the beer to which they had been accustomed in England and Holland, they had an abundance of pure, sweet water close at hand.

Religion always was prominent in their thoughts and conduct. Probably family prayers were customarily held at least once a day and in many of their homes twice.[15] Public worship on the Sabbath [16] was maintained regularly and was expected to be attended by all who had no proper reason for absence, yet there is no good ground for supposing that religious obligations were enforced in any such a narrow and oppressive manner as often has been intimated. It is uncertain when they built their first proper meeting-house but it seems to have been in 1637.[17] Up to that time they probably continued to hold their public worship in the block-house, with occasional services in the "common house." It was in the latter that Robert Cushman, during his visit in the autumn of 1621, delivered his address on self-love, which — although it was no more a sermon than any one of Elder Brewster's customary addresses on the Sabbath — has been called "the first sermon preached in New England and the corner-stone of American literature." They had no Sunday-school and even the custom of holding a prayer-meeting in the middle of the week was unknown among them.[18]

As has been suggested already, the version of the Bible in use among them, although they may have had copies of any one of several, — the Bishops' Bible, or Coverdale's translation or even Tyndale's or Wyclif's, — is by far most likely to have been the Genevan. Either of these sounds rugged and quaint to modern ears, but, whichever they had, it was a great comfort to them. We know that they sang out of the even more quaint, and positively uncouth, contents of the Book of Psalms, compiled by Henry Ainsworth, the former friend of some among them in Amsterdam, a book in which the psalms are arranged for metrical use. But it was the best they had, if not also the best book of the sort then in existence.

It would be of great interest if we knew the order of public worship which the Pilgrims followed at this time. But we can only infer what it was from what we know that it had been a few years earlier in Holland, and what we also know that it was in their own colony only a few years later.

In a book written by Rev. Richard Clifton after the Pilgrims had removed from Amsterdam to Leyden occurs an outline of the order of service in the church of which Francis Johnson was pastor in the former city. It is as follows :[19]

1. Prayer and thanksgiving by the pastor or teacher.
2. Reading of two or three chapters of the Bible, with brief explanation of the same, as the time may serve.
3. The singing of some of the Psalms of David.
4. A sermon — that is, the pastor or teacher expounds and enforces some passage of the Scripture.
5. The singing again of some of the Psalms of David.
6. The Sacraments are administered — that is, the

Lord's Supper on stated Sundays, and baptism whenever there might be a candidate.
7. Collection is then made, as each one is able, for the support of the officers, and the poor.

There is much probability that this order was that customary for substance in the early Congregational churches, and that it was followed by the church of the Pilgrims in Leyden and also after their settlement at Plymouth.

Additional light is thrown upon the subject by a passage in Governor Winthrop's famous journal in which he is describing a visit made at Plymouth by him in 1632. He says : [20]

On the Lord's day [in the forenoon] there was a sacrament, which they did partake in; and, in the afternoon, Mr. Roger Williams, (according to their custom) propounded a question, to which the pastor, Mr. Smith, spake briefly; then Mr. Williams prophesied; and after[ward] the Governour [Bradford] of Plimouth spake to the question; after him the Elder [Brewster]; then some two or three more of the congregation. Then the Elder desired the Governour of Massachusetts [Winthrop] and Mr. [Rev. John] Wilson to speak to it, which they did. When this was ended, the Deacon, Mr. Fuller, put the congregation in mind of their duty of contribution; whereupon the Governour and all the rest went down to the deacon's seat, and put into the box, and then returned.

It hardly is to be understood that prayer, singing, and the reading of Scripture were omitted upon this occasion because Governor Winthrop does not specify them. Doubtless they all were given place as usual and his neglect to record them must have been because he knew that any probable reader of his diary would perceive that they were to be taken for granted, mention being made only of the more striking portions of the service. Apparently they gave more prominence to the sermon than we give it and used it for the explanation and enforcement of Scriptural doctrine more than is now common, although they certainly did not neglect due consideration of Christian virtues and practical duties. Sometimes also they seem to have listened to several successive speakers during a single service.

Such, evidently, were some of the characteristic features of the early life of the colony. Compared with our modern usages, or even with their own life a generation or two later, it seems monotonous and confined, to say the least. But the Pilgrims had won their freedom, for which to them no sacrifices were too great, and after their own quiet manner they must have taken much substantial enjoyment in their new home, in spite of their sometimes hard conditions. The common impression that they were stern and morose, destitute of the sense of humor and always inclined to gloomy views and indifferent to the graces of life, is exaggerated. Certainly their history and circumstances were such as would have rendered any thoughtful men or women who ever lived grave and sedate, more intent upon the realities of this life and the life to come than upon comparative trivialities, however innocent and pleasant in themselves; and such the Pilgrims for the most part undoubtedly were. But conspicuous fortitude, energy, and Christian faith like theirs do not render people gloomy, and it is safe to believe that in their domestic life and their mutual friendly intercourse there was abundant cheerfulness, and even genuine merry-making, whenever their circumstances were not too depressing.

Surely such a study of them and their ways, which, imperfect although it is, must be reasonably true to the facts, reveals them as a company of men and women of whom their children well may be proud. Their life, although primitive and unadorned, was dignified, honorable, and ennobling, and has proved to be of world-wide service. They cherished the highest, holiest purposes. They demonstrated their sincerity by their sacrifices. Moreover, they were as ready to move forward along inviting lines of commendable social progress as they were careful to hold fast by what they had proved safe and serviceable. In spite of what now seems to many their extreme conservatism, their whole history shows that they were not among the conservatives but the progressives of their times.

CHAPTER XXV.

DISTINCTIONS BETWEEN THE PLYMOUTH AND BAY COLONIES.

MENTION already has been made of several attempts to settle upon Massachusetts Bay, and there had been others. In the same year, 1622, in which Weston had sent his colony to Wessagusset, now Weymouth,[1] a trading station had been established by Thomas and John Gray and Walter Knight at Nantasket, or Hull, which had become permanent in 1624.[2] Robert Gorges had tried vainly to colonize at Wessagusset in 1623.[3] Samuel Maverick had occupied Winnisimmet, now Chelsea, in 1624, moving to Noddle's Island, now East Boston, in 1627.[4] Thomas Walford had established himself at Mishawum, the present Charlestown, in 1624 or 1625,[5] and in the same year Mount

Wollaston had been settled by Captain Wollaston's expedition, Thomas Morton and William Blackstone remaining after most of the company had withdrawn,[6] and the latter soon, probably in 1625, moving over to Shawmut, now Boston.[7] Other small beginnings also had been made by 1628 where Dorchester, Watertown, Salem, Gloucester, and Dover, N. H., now are. But no proper colony had been established successfully.

On September 6, 1628, however, John Endicott landed from the ship George at Salem[8] with a considerable company, some of whom settled there, while others established themselves at Charlestown. It is said that by the autumn of 1629 about a hundred persons were in the latter settlement.[9] Other ships and immigrants followed the George during the same year. On June 9, 1630, the first shipload of John Winthrop's company reached Nantasket in the Mary & John,[10] and on June 22 Winthrop in person and accompanied by another portion of his company landed at Salem. Five days later Winthrop visited Charlestown and examined that region and liked it so well that he decided to settle there.[11] But it did not prove as favorable a situation as was expected, and the lack of good water and food sufficient for so many soon scattered his colonists.

Some moved to Roxbury, others to Medford, and Winthrop himself, with the Rev. Mr. Wilson and most of his congregation, over to Boston. From that time, in spite of one or two periods of temporary hardships, the Massachusetts Bay Colony, to which all these settlements fairly belonged, continued to increase and prosper. It outnumbered the Plymouth Colony from the outset and quickly surpassed it in prominence. But in some most important particulars the latter exerted the more controlling influence. To narrate the career of the Bay Colony, interesting although it is, is not included in the purpose of this book. But, in view of the fact that even to the present day the two colonies often are confused in popular thought and speech, it is important that the actual distinctions between them should be indicated briefly.

First, then, it should be remembered that the Plymouth Colony was a company of Separatists and Congregationalists, who revolted from the Church of England because of its many abuses and felt obliged in conscience to sever their connection with it. The ruling purpose of their separation and of their subsequent emigrations from England to Holland and from Holland to America was to obtain and maintain their religious liberty. They seem to have been content with the material conditions of their lives in England and probably would not have left their native land in order to better themselves financially. So far as they can be said to have prospered at all in a worldly sense in Holland, they were grateful, but did not forget their spiritual aims or come to regard them as of minor importance. Moreover, after reaching Plymouth, their zeal in founding their colony and in farming, trading, and sending back fish and skins to England was due more to the necessity of self-preservation and to their obligation to the Adventurers, without whose aid, no matter how grudgingly rendered, they could not have crossed the ocean at all, than to any ruling ambition to acquire wealth. It is true that among them, even on the Mayflower, were some who had little sympathy with their spiritual beliefs and aspirations and chiefly sought adventures, wealth, or both. This was inevitable, but — excepting Allerton, and he was no exception for some years at first — not only the leaders but also the great majority of the other members of their colony were both devout and godly in life and were stanch, intelligent Separatists, who deliberately were risking everything for the sake of freedom in matters religious and ecclesiastical.

In the Bay Colony the case was quite different. This colony was definitely Puritan in distinction from Separatist. Rev. Francis Higginson, of Salem, wrote thus:

> We will not say as the Separatists were wont to say at their leaving of England, Farewel Babylon! Farewel Rome! But we will say, Farewel Dear England! Farewel the Church of God in England, and all the Christian friends there! We do not go to New England as Separatists from the Church of England; though we cannot but separate from the Corruptions in it: But we go to practise the positive Part of Church Reformation, and propagate the Gospel in America.[12]

And Winthrop's company published in London, just before they sailed for America, a treatise, *The hvmble Reqvest of his Majestie's loyall Subjects*, etc., in which they speak of themselves

> As those who esteem it our honour to call the *Church of England* from whence wee rise, our deare mother; and cannot part from our native countrie where she specially resideth, without much sadnes of heart and many tears in our eyes.[13]

They were simply Puritans. They were

grieved by the corruptions of the English Church, but they meant to reëstablish it, purified of its evils, in their colony. They were not Separatists and still less Congregationalists, and did not mean to become such. Circumstances soon proved too much for them,[14] but so far was their original purpose from favoring separation that, when Rev. Ralph Smith applied to come over with some of the early colonists of Salem and the governor and council learned that he was disposed towards Separatism, they at first decided to forbid his joining them and later, upon changing their minds, directed that "vnless hee wilbe conformable to or [our] governmt, yow suffer him not to remaine wthin the limitts of or graunt."[15] As has been related, Smith soon found his way to Plymouth — there is evidence that he was forced to leave Salem[16] — and became the pastor of the Pilgrim church. When the Bay colonists came over they meant to have a reformed and purified church, but nevertheless the State Church. Naturally, therefore, and speedily, as early as May 28, 1631, the General Court of the Massachusetts Colony voted

That for time to come *noe man shalbe admitted to the freedome of this body polliticke, but such as are members of some of the churches within the lymitts of the same.*[17]

It had the right to pass such a vote and there were some apparently good reasons for it, although it led to serious evils. It should be remembered, too, — the name General Court being misleading, — that this action was not that of the legislature of a State or even a colony, but of the stockholders and managers of a financial corporation.[18]

This must not be forgotten. It is quite true that many of the patrons and leaders of the Bay Colony also were actuated by religious motives, some of them prominently, and meant to exemplify Puritanism as they were not allowed to in England. Yet the whole scheme of the

Bay Colony was primarily commercial and grew out of the purpose to establish a strong, prosperous trading colony and to do this so quickly as to outwit John Oldham and anticipate him in occupying permanently the region bordering on Massachusetts Bay, which he was aiming to settle in coöperation with the Gorges family.[19] So far as there is any difference in the significance of the records which relate to this subject, it is due to the fact that some writers took one view of the dominant purpose of the colony, others the other view, all being alike interested in its success. But a comparison of them seems to exhibit the commercial motive in the strongest light.

The effect of this vote of the General Court was to unite the State, so far as any existed, with the Church. "Church and State were one; and the church dominated the state. The franchise was an incident to church membership."[20] But at Plymouth this was not the fact.[21] So far as is known, even Miles Standish never joined the church,[22] and there is some ground for believing that he was, at least nominally, a Roman Catholic. And in reply to a charge made by the convicted slanderer, Lyford, that "if ther come over any honest men that are not of ye separation, they will quickly distast them," Governor Bradford and others declared that "they had many amongst them that they liked well of, and were glad of their company; and should be glad of any such like that should come amongst them." [23]

It already has been shown, and therefore need only be repeated, that these non-Separatists were regular legal members of the colony. This suggests that, as a result of the difference in reference to the union of Church and State, the Plymouth Colony was a democracy but the Bay Colony an aristocracy. This also was due quite as much, doubtless, and perhaps more, to the fact that, while most of the Plymouth Pilgrims were of comparatively humble origin in England, only three or four being known to us as having been of gentle birth, although several others were men of university training and much culture, the Bay Colony contained a comparatively large number of representatives of English aristocratic families.[24]

One other point of difference, already hinted at, must be mentioned. The Plymouth Colony was distinguished for liberality and tolerance. The occurrences which so often are quoted indiscriminately against both as proofs of bigotry and intolerance belong to the history of the Bay Colony. Oldham and Lyford truly were expelled from Plymouth in 1625 for public and extravagant offenses, but they had rendered themselves unendurable, and even Oldham was welcomed back as soon as he was willing to behave himself. Not long afterwards Roger Williams lived among the Pilgrims for a year or two, kindly treated and allowed free speech, even being permitted to act as assistant to Mr. Smith, the pastor, although his peculiar views generally were distrusted.[25] The Plymouth men also refused to persecute the Quakers afterwards, several of them being deprived of colonial offices for this reason.[26]

But in the Bay Colony Thomas Morton was punished severely in 1630 on trivial, trumped-up charges in order to get rid of him, which, in spite of his many and serious actual offenses, was a grave injustice.[27] Philip Ratcliff,[28] in 1631, was whipped, had his ears cut off, and was fined £40 and banished for denouncing the church authorities and the Salem magistrates, and there occurred other similar cases. At about the same time two prominent men in Salem, named Brown,[29] were summoned before the governor and council for objecting to the disuse of the English prayer-book; and, being compelled to choose between the prayer-book and the colony, they preferred the former and were sent back to

England. Troubles with Mrs. Hutchinson, Roger Williams, and others occurred afterwards and on a larger scale, agitating the whole colony, and are too well known to need detailed mention here.

The Plymouth Pilgrims, then, were Separatists and Congregationalists from the outset, but the Bay colonists came over merely as non-separating Puritans. The former fled from bitter persecution in England; the latter came away with the approval and indorsement of the civil authorities. The former came to America definitely in pursuit of religious liberty; the latter sought additional religious liberty, but also were distinctively a commercial corporation with a business aim. The former severed the Church from the State; but the latter united and, in a sense, identified them. The former colony was a democracy, the latter an aristocracy. The Pilgrims were conspicuous for liberality and tolerance; the Bay Puritans too often were undeniably intolerant. The Puritans of the Bay were earnest and generally noble Christian men and women. The fault of their intolerance, it is true, lay not with them so much as with their age. It was as characteristic of England as it was of their colony. They only acted as most good people then thought it right, and even necessary, to act; and, with all their faults, they did a grand work and can afford to have the truth about them told. But the Plymouth Pilgrims were in advance of the age. They had risen to a higher level of charity and tolerance, and they exhibited a type of Christianity then, and too often even now, as rare as it is beautiful and honorable.

CHAPTER XXVI.

SUBSEQUENT DEVELOPMENT OF CONGREGATIONALISM.

OUR attention necessarily has been fixed largely upon the material side of the growth of the Plymouth Colony, because for some years it was uncertain whether the enterprise would live or die. It is not to be inferred, however, that even during this period of struggle and distress the Pilgrims were forgetful of their determination to rule themselves, under God, in ecclesiastical and religious affairs. But it was almost ten years, as has been said, before they obtained an ordained minister, and it was nearly nine years before the second church in New England — that in Salem, organized, or completed in its organization, August 6, 1629 — was formed.[1] Thus left to themselves, they practically were forced by circumstances to adhere to their theory of an independent, self-governing church, as otherwise they might not have been. Moreover, they not only learned to believe more firmly than ever in this theory, but also, when the time came, they served as a notable example of its excellence in practice. Evidence to this effect is on record. For example, in 1644 Mr. W. Rathband, in his *Brief Narration of some Church Courses, etc.*, wrote that he had been told by "Mr. W. [possibly Winslow], an eminent man of the Church at *Plimmoth* . . . that the rest of the Churches in *New Eng.* came at first to them at *Plimmoth* to crave their direction in Church courses, and made them their pattern."[2]

The Bay colonists also felt the controlling force of the conditions of their new life. At first, owing to their predisposition against Congregationalism and even against Separatism, and also to certain reports about the Pilgrims which had reached them in England, they were prepared to distrust the ecclesiastical methods of the latter. But when Dr. Samuel Fuller, a deacon in the Plymouth church, had explained these, — during his visit to the Bay in 1629, already mentioned, almost as soon as the Salem colonists had arrived, — Endicott, their leader, became fully convinced that the Pilgrims had been misunderstood. Thenceforth, therefore, the example of the Plymouth church had its due weight.

Moreover — and it is somewhat surprising that the results should have come to pass so soon — the Salem colony had been founded less than two years, and whatever addition it received from Winthrop's company had been ashore only about a month when it had altered its former views so radically that it actually formed an independent church for itself, and not only elected and ordained its pastor and teacher, but did so in spite of the fact that each of them formerly had been ordained in England.[3] Furthermore, those in control also recognized the fellowship of the churches by inviting the Plymouth church to be present at the succeeding ordination of elders and deacons; and Governor Bradford and others, although detained by stress of weather, arrived and in time for him to give the right hand of fellowship.[4] The action of the Salem men was not only Separatism but Congregationalism; and, although it caused outspoken alarm among patrons of the colony in England, it was imitated by others as new churches were needed and organized.

But the freedom of modern Congregationalism had not yet been attained. The ruling eldership continued to exist and to exert its abnormal and cramping influence. In the Plymouth church there was but one elder during its early life, William Brewster, and he guided his fellow members so wisely and so much by the mere weight of his exalted personal character that, although the eldership received honor through him, it was the man rather than the official who exerted the influence. But in the churches of the Bay Colony the ruling elders were conceded and exercised a domination quite inconsistent with the proper liberty of the other members.

So great was the authority yielded to them that in Rev. Richard Mather's volume, *Church-Government and Church-Covenant discussed*, *etc.*, printed in 1643, it is declared that although the power of government in the church should be given "neither all to the people excluding the Presbytery, nor all to the Presbytery excluding the people," [5] nevertheless the reason why the presbyters or elders can do nothing without the consent of the people is that when they do their duty the people ought to assent to it, and "if any man should in such a case willfully dissent, the Church ought to deale with such an one, for not consenting." [6] That is, the elders should rule the church and, if any lay member should object, he should be disciplined. Some individuals and some churches held a more liberal theory, but this prevailed commonly. The famous Cambridge Platform, drawn up between 1648 and 1651, takes the same ground in substance.

Moreover, the power of the elders tended to increase rather than to diminish from the first. This was a natural result of the old endeavor — a characteristic of Henry Barrowe's and Francis Johnson's scheme of church government, which has been described earlier — to manage a Congregational church on a Presbyterian theory. As the churches multiplied, of course the influence of this theory was extended, and as the Bay Colony soon became much more extensive, numerous, wealthy, and influential than the Plymouth Colony, and in time absorbed it, the type of Congregationalism in the Bay Colony became dominant generally, especially as the Plymouth church still retained the formal eldership. Both the direct testimony and the indirect

— including that drawn from criticisms upon the New England way — show that this type was not truly democratic. It was not such Presbyterianism as had become controlling temporarily in England, but it was not Congregationalism. Indeed, half a century later, after some churches had ceased to elect ruling elders, their power remained in the hands of the pastor, whose veto outweighed the vote of the whole church.[7] Meanwhile, in 1662, the Half-way Covenant, admitting orthodox and moral baptized, but not necessarily converted, persons to all church privileges except the Lord's Supper, had been adopted, and grave and widespread demoralization had resulted.[8]

This condition of matters continued until 1705.[9] In that year the Boston Association of Ministers adopted sixteen proposals, which they submitted to the other similar associations in the State for approval. The most important of these proposals involved the membership of all ministers in associations; the union by delegates of these associations in an annual meeting; the establishment of a standing council, composed of the members of this delegated association and of a proper number of other delegates, apparently to be laymen, representing the churches; and the control of all church affairs throughout the State by this standing council. This practically meant the destruction of whatever measure of independence still remained to the individual churches. In Connecticut three years later, in 1708, a synod met at Saybrook, consisting of twelve ministers and four laymen chosen by the ministers of all the churches and authorized and summoned by the General Court. It reaffirmed the Savoy Confession and the Heads of Agreement adopted April 6, 1691, by the leading Congregational and Presbyterian ministers of London, and drew up the famous Saybrook Platform, which provided a system of consociations for the government of ecclesiastical affairs in that State. This was another step, and an equally important one, in the direction of limiting the freedom of the churches. These measures at once awakened opposition and criticism, although they long continued to possess influence, and Consociationism still exists in parts of Connecticut, although in name more than in substance.

They helped to prepare the way, however, for the final step in the process of developing ancient Congregationalism into essentially its modern form. In 1710 Rev. John Wise,[10] pastor of the church in Ipswich, Mass., gave to the public a little book called *The Churches Quarrel Espoused; or a Reply in Satyre, to certain Proposals made*, and in 1717 he brought out another book entitled, *A Vindication of the Government of New England Churches, Drawn from Antiquity; the Light of Nature; Holy Scripture; its Noble Nature; and from the Dignity Divine Providence has put upon it.* These books were read widely and had a great influence. It is believed by some that probably their author only meant to recall the churches to the ground taken in the Cambridge Platform, but he started a movement which carried them much further, aroused the laity to the danger of being deprived of their rights, and led by degrees in due time to the abolition of the ruling eldership and the recognition both of the democratic character of the government of each church and also of its independence, yet in genuine mutual fellowship.[11] Thus the spirit of the Plymouth Pilgrims at last became that of New England and now is that of Congregationalists throughout our country.

It has been proper, and in a sense necessary, to outline thus the development of Congregationalism in times subsequent to the period naturally covered by this volume, because the success of the undertaking attempted by the Pilgrims, that of founding "a free Church in a free State," cannot otherwise be understood fairly. They "builded better than they knew," indeed. The later development of their ideas of spiritual and ecclesiastical truth has proved to be along the very lines which they laid down. Their purpose in leaving England was attained by them, and it also has been fulfilled by their spiritual children, of whom many are also their descendants in the flesh, more richly than they ever can have dreamed possible.

CHAPTER XXVII.

CONCLUSION.

THE object of our study now has been accomplished. The rise and progress of the Pilgrim movement has been described, so far at least, it is hoped, as to make plain something of the exalted character of the men and women whom preëminently the world has agreed to call the Pilgrims, and also the prominent facts in their civil and ecclesiastical history. After the Plymouth Colony had become established successfully, had secured its financial independence, and had witnessed and assisted at the inauguration of the practice of its own peculiar ecclesiastical theory in the young sister colony at the Bay, the history of its members, as Pilgrims, fairly may be said to have closed. Their pilgrimage was ended and its reward had been won. Out of their sorrows and perils they emerged at last into liberty and peace. They were not faultless, yet it would be difficult to point to any other community on record in which more of real happiness was experienced generally than in theirs. Their life was simple, natural, and laborious, but, after the difficulties inherent in the firm establishment of the colony had been overcome at last, it was not one of hardship. They gradually attained a high degree of material comfort and some of them enjoyed what for the times was moderate luxury.

They maintained steadily their lofty intellectual, moral, and religious standards and soon exerted an enlightening influence upon the world out of all proportion to the smallness of their colony. Unreasoning praise would be peculiarly inappropriate to them, but the discriminating judgment of the ages is ranking them high. Long ago Christendom learned to admire and respect them and it is safe to believe that in the future they will be honored even more than in the past. Indeed, it only recently has begun to be perceived intelligently how great a debt is due to them and how noble and far-reaching the influence of their careers has been. In 1692, about seventy years after the settlement at Plymouth, — so that the period of its separate life must have coincided closely with that of some of its earliest native-born members,[1] — the colony was united with the neighboring colony of Massachusetts Bay.[2] But, as has been suggested already, the larger colony had modeled itself upon the smaller in some most important particulars, so that much of the power and influence of Massachusetts ever since has been due conspicuously to the Plymouth people.

Moreover, the success of the colony proved to be the turning-point of the feeble and waning flow of English colonization in North America. Says Governor Hutchinson, "the ablest historian who wrote in this country before the Revolution ": —

The settlement of this colony occasioned the settlement of Massachusetts Bay, which was the source of all the other colonies of New England. Virginia was in a dying state, and seemed to revive and flourish from the example of New England. I am not preserving from oblivion the names of heroes whose chief merit is the overthrow of cities, provinces and empires, but the names of the founders of a flourishing town and colony, if not of the whole British empire in America.[3]

What nobler or more instructive panorama can be found in the whole broad field of human history than that composed of the successive episodes in the career of the Pilgrims? We have seen them at first, generally humble and obscure, cruelly oppressed in their native England and most bitterly persecuted in respect to that which to all noble souls is dearest, their right to worship God as their consciences dictated. We have seen them meekly yet firmly loyal to divine truth, as they understood it, and calmly yet sadly consenting to exile themselves from home and country lest they be disloyal to the Almighty. We have seen them, pursued and harassed like shameless criminals, unable to remain in England yet long forbidden to depart, and at last only contemptuously allowed to banish themselves; incurring poverty, imprisonment, the perils of the sea, and the discomforts of a strange and uncongenial land; and gaining a temporary resting place in Amsterdam only to find the dissensions of their countrymen almost as perilous to their peace and safety as the tyranny of their rulers had been at home.

We have seen them, again removed and settled for a few years in Leyden, humbly and patiently industrious, law-abiding, winning the confidence of the people and the praise of the public authorities, enjoying religious freedom, and working out their ecclesiastical theories for the benefit of coming generations. We have seen them even then hampered by extreme poverty, alarmed by the perils of their children, and disappointed in the failure of their great hopes of being able to preserve their existence as a body and of securing for their theories of spiritual and ecclesiastical truth an advantageous and permanent opportunity of successful illustration. We have seen them, therefore, once more exiling themselves bravely and venturing this time not into a well-known, even though to them unfamiliar, land but beyond the confines of civilization itself. We have seen them, still hindered by grievous penury, forced to divide themselves as a body in twain, hampered by the falseness or negligence of those who had pledged them sufficient and immediate aid, delayed by treachery, sickened and alarmed by the perils of the deep, and reaching at last not their intended destination but an unknown, bleak, inhospitable shore, and in the dead of winter.

We have seen them exploring patiently, establishing their colony feebly and slowly, and sickening and suffering uncomplainingly until every other member of their company had succumbed to death and had been laid in a necessarily hidden grave. We have seen them starving by inches, annoyed and actually endangered by visitors whose hungry mouths they had to fill out of their insufficient, precarious, and failing supplies of food, threatened by the Indian natives, and imperiled by the recklessness and incompetency of settlers of other and newer colonies. We have seen them forced to allow the settlement among themselves of many who had no sympathy with their spirit or purpose, who sought to create dissensions and who had to be controlled with a strong hand. We have seen them deprived for years of the sight of the relatives and friends whom they had expected to follow them soon from Holland, and unable for nearly a decade to enjoy the precious fellowship and services of a Christian minister and the holy comfort of the sacraments. We have seen them neglected and even meanly reproached by those at home who had promised to supply permanently their material needs, hampered by the miserable mismanagement of the Merchant Adventurers, and forced at last either to assume the whole financial burden of their undertaking at a heavy cost and a heavier risk of total failure or else to lose all which they had invested or accomplished.

But also we have seen in them examples of sagacity, patience, versatility in resource, fortitude, persistence, and consecration such as never have been surpassed. We have seen not only strong men but also tender women and little children sharing the burdens and perils of their common experience with unconscious but not less lofty heroism. We have seen material success and prosperity triumphantly won in spite of the most adverse conditions. We have seen an almost peerless devotion to God and a self-sacrificing missionary spirit. We have seen an evident, absolute absorption in the effort to learn and obey the divine will, which rarely has been paralleled among men. We have seen a tolerance, a charity, and a degree of spiritual enlightenment far in advance of their times and which the Christian world in general even now hardly can be said to have attained. We have seen an intelligent, orderly, generally self-consistent and always peaceable and harmonious development of a theory of church existence and government which many now believe, as they believed, to be at once most natural and most Scriptural, and which — partly through its direct, acknowledged influence, exerted by hundreds of thousands of Christians in various branches of the earthly church, and partly through its less evident and admitted but undeniable general influence upon Christian bodies differently named and governed — soon justified itself as well as the toils and sacrifices of the Pilgrims and of their fellow believers, who elsewhere and otherwise have striven for the same great object.

The Pilgrims long ago rested from their labors and entered into their reward. But their works still follow them. The multitude of their descendants in the flesh does well to honor their memory, and the far greater and ever increasing host of their spiritual children never will cease to reverence them. But even reverence will be empty unless accompanied by imitation. Both the need and the opportunity of the spirit of the Pilgrims still continue among us.

NOTES.

CHAPTER I.

1. Neal, History of the Puritans [Harpers, 1844], i, 30–1. J. R. Green, A Short History of the English People [Harpers, 1888], 267.

2. Green, A Short History of the English People, 349. Massingberd, English Reformation [Longmans, Green & Co., 1866], 285. Lord Herbert of Cherbury, History of England under Henry VIII [A. Murray, 1870], 478. Skeats, History of Free Churches in England [A. Miall, 1869], 2.

3. Neal, History of the Puritans, i, 34–6.

4. Ibid. i, 57. Green, A Short History of the English People, 368.

5. Neal, History of the Puritans, i, 59. Green, A Short History of the English People, 362.

6. Neal, History of the Puritans, i, 60.

7. Ibid. i, 66.

8. Ibid. i, 64.

9. Ibid. i, 71, 81–2, 216. Green, A Short History of the English People, 376.

10. Tulloch, English Puritanism and its Leaders [Blackwoods, 1861], 15. Froude, History of England [Scribners, 1870], xii, 582. Green, A Short History of the English People, 376. John Fiske, Beginnings of New England [Houghton, Mifflin & Co., 1889], 60.

11. Neal, History of the Puritans, i, 74, 89, 137. Strype, Annals, iii, 183–4. Green, A Short History of the English People, 408.

12. Neal, History of the Puritans, i, 182. Green, A Short History of the English People, 405.

13. Neal, History of the Puritans, i, 76, 112, 127, 158. Massingberd, English Reformation, 491-3. Green, A Short History of the English People, 468-72.

14. Neal, History of the Puritans, i, 86, 149.

15. Ibid. i, 93, 97.

16. Ibid. i, 148.

17. Ibid. i, 134-5.

18. Ibid. i, 147, 179.

19. Ibid. i, 131.

20. Ibid. i, 104, 176.

21. Ibid. i, 116.

22. Ibid. i, 83, 116, 146-7, 159, 165-6, 168, 179.

23. Ibid. i, 146.

24. Ibid. i, 102-3, 146.

25. Ibid. i, 146, 165, 173, 181.

26. Ibid. i, 86.

27. Ibid. i, 126-7, 154, 215.

28. Ibid. i, 232. Tulloch, English Puritanism and its Leaders, 37.

CHAPTER II.

1. Blomefield, History of the County of Norfolk, iii, 282, 291. Quoted in H. M. Dexter's Congregationalism as Seen in the Literature of the Last Three Hundred Years [Harpers, 1880], 72, note. Froude, History of England, vii, 270, 413.

2. Blomefield, History of the County of Norfolk, iii, 337.

3. Neal, History of the Puritans, i, 66. Rev. John Brown, D.D., mentions one at Bocking in 1551 and thinks that there were others of earlier dates. See Tercentenary Tracts, No. VI, Congregationalism Old and New

[Congregational Union of England and Wales, 1893], 9, 10. But it does not seem clear that any of them were sufficiently well organized or permanent to be considered regular.

4. Neal, History of the Puritans, i, 66. Brown, Tercentenary Tracts, No. VI, 12.

5. Neal, History of the Puritans, i, 104–5.

6. Ibid. i, 106, etc., 214.

7. Ibid. i, 106. Professor Williston Walker, PH.D., The Heads of Agreement, etc. [Proceedings of American Society of Church History, 1891], 32.

8. Skeats, History of the Free Churches in England, 23. Dexter, Congregationalism in Literature, 69–70, 101.

9. Neal, History of the Puritans, i, 198. Strype, Annals, iv, 174. John Robinson, Justification of Separation, 460. Dexter, Congregationalism in Literature, 114–15, 631–4. Dr. Brown — Tercentenary Tracts, No. VI, 13, etc. — quotes Thomas Lever's testimony that there was a church in London in 1559 and also refers to Richard Fitz's church as probably formed in the Bridewell Prison in 1567 or a little later. That these companies existed is clear. The fact needing to be established is that they, or either of them, professed distinctive Congregationalist principles instead of being Congregationalists merely so far as their independence, the necessary result of their circumstances, rendered them like Congregationalists. This fact does not yet appear to have been proved.

10. Sir S. D'Ewes, Journal of all the Parliaments during the Reign of Queen Elizabeth, etc., 517. Quoted by Dexter, Congregationalism in Literature, 631, note.

11. History of the Puritans, i, 149.

12. Constitutional History of England, ii, 296.

13. On the other hand Green, Short History of the English People, edition of 1894, pp. 1177–8, thinks,

and quotes Bacon in his support, that by the end of the reign they had been practically suppressed. But the weight of the evidence is the other way.

14. Baptists, Unitarians, and others are Congregationalists in respect to polity.

CHAPTER III.

1. Dexter, Congregationalism in Literature, 61–128, furnishes a careful study of the man, his theories, etc.

2. See chapter ii, note 1.

CHAPTER IV.

1. Dexter, Congregationalism in Literature, 407, 459–60.

2. Those of Robert Browne, for example, mentioned in chapter ii.

3. Their titles are as follows: 2. Oh read ouer D. Iohn Bridges, etc.: Or an Epitome of the fyrste Booke, etc.; 3. Certaine Minerall and Metaphisicall School points, etc.; 4. Hay any worke for Cooper, etc.; 5. The Protestatyon of Martin Marprelat, etc.; 6. Theses Martinianæ, etc.; 7. The iust censure and reproofe of Martin Iunior, etc. The first and second must not be confused with each other through the similarity of their titles.

4. Dr. Dexter proposed this theory. Congregationalism in Literature, 192–201.

5. Ibid. 208–10.

6. Ibid. 209–10.

7. Copping and Thacker are said to have answered " cruel Judge Popham" thus: —

"My Lord, your face we fear not,
"And for your threats we care not,
"And to come to your read service we dare not."

Bradford, Dialogue in Young, Chronicles, 427.

8. Dexter, Congregationalism in Literature, 208.

9. Young, Chronicles of the Pilgrims [Little & Brown, 1844], 427.

10. Dexter, Congregationalism in Literature, 211-45.

11. Ibid. 211-45.

12. Ibid. 246-51.

13. A public service was held in the City Temple on April 6, 1893, and an open-air meeting at the main gate into Hyde Park, where the "Tyburn Tree," that is, Tyburn gallows, used to stand, on April 8. The attendance at the latter service was estimated at 15,000 persons.

CHAPTER V.

1. B. Evans, Early English Baptists, i, 202. Brook, Lives of the Puritans, ii, 196. J. Ivimey, History of English Baptists, i, 114. A. Taylor, History of English General Baptists, etc., i, 67. All quoted by Dexter, Congregationalism in Literature, 312, note.

2. Founders of New Plymouth [J. R. Smith, 1854], 20-1.

3. See his letter in article "King James at Scrooby," by Dr. E. E. Hale, New England Magazine, September, 1889.

4. Dexter, article "Footprints of Pilgrims in England," Sabbath at Home, March, 1867.

5. Founders of New Plymouth, 20.

6. Itinerary, i, 36.

7. Dexter, article "Footprints of Pilgrims in England," Sabbath at Home, March, 1867.

8. Bradford, History of Plymouth Plantations [Collections of Massachusetts Historical Society, 4th series, vol. iii], 411-12, notes.

9. Article "Round About Scrooby," New England Magazine, September, 1889. Hunter, Founders of New Plymouth, 21.

10. See account in The Congregationalist of August 13, 1891.

CHAPTER VI.

1. Dexter, article " Footprints of Pilgrims in England," Sabbath at Home, March, 1867.
2. Hunter, Founders of New Plymouth, 61.
3. History, 409.
4. Encyclopædia Britannica [Scribners, 1885], Post-office.
5. Dexter, " Footprints of Pilgrims in England," Sabbath at Home, March, 1867.
6. History, 410.
7. Ibid. 411.
8. Ibid. 412-13.
9. Ibid. 30-8, 31, note.
10. Ibid. 447.
11. Ibid. 339, note.
12. Plymouth Church Records, written by Nathaniel Morton, secretary of the colony. But the late Charles Deane, editor of Bradford's History, accepted April 28, 1643, as probably correct.
13. See Deane's preface to the 1856 edition of Bradford's History. Dexter, Mourt's Relation [J. K. Wiggin, 1865], 14, note.
14. Founders of New Plymouth, 107, 110.

CHAPTER VII.

1. History, 10.
2. Bradford, in Young, Chronicles, 453. Hunter, Founders of New Plymouth, 40-6.

3. Bradford, History, 18, 20–1, 205. Dexter, Congregationalism in Literature, 359–410.

4. Founders of New Plymouth, 93.

5. According to testimony of Baron Elsivier and Professor Pluygers. Referred to by Dexter, article "The Pilgrims in Leyden," New England Magazine, September, 1889.

6. The house now standing where the large house then stood is called the Pesijns Hof, after Jan Pesijn, who founded there an asylum for aged and poor married people in 1683.

7. University Registers. The date is September 15, 1615.

8. For example, he became exempt from the jurisdiction of the magistrates of the city and entitled to receive, free of town or state duties, half a ton — 126 English gallons — of beer every month and about ten gallons of wine every three months.

9. Young, Chronicles, 492.

10. The following is a summary of the arguments. In proof that Robinson had reference to progress and liberality in general it is urged that

(*a*) His words must be given their natural meaning;

(*b*) His biographer's [Ashton's] testimony as to his character establishes a probability that he meant to be understood in the broadest sense; and,

(*c*) This interpretation harmonizes with the immediately succeeding sentences of his address.

In proof that he referred only to church government it is urged that this interpretation is the more consistent

(*a*) With his often expressed ecclesiastical opinions;

(*b*) With the conditions of the occasion of the utterance;

(*c*) With the circumstances in which it was reported by Edward Winslow, through whom it has come to us;

(*d*) With the common understanding of it in New England for a century and a half after Winslow published his report of the address; and,

(*e*) With several other closely following and unmistakably significant sentences of the address.

For a full examination of the subject see Dexter, Congregationalism in Literature, 403, etc.

11. See account in The Congregationalist of August 13, 1891.

CHAPTER VIII.

1. Founders of New Plymouth, 128, 131.
2. Ibid. 19, 72–3, 128–31.
3. In Holland at this time betrothal had to be registered officially like marriage.
4. Hunter, Founders of New Plymouth, 17, 116–17.
5. Worksop Parish Records. Hunter, Founders of New Plymouth, 126.
6. History, 12.
7. Leyden Records, quoted by Dexter, Congregationalism in Literature, 383.
8. Founders of New Plymouth, 124.
9. Dexter, Mourt's Relation, xviii, etc.
10. Hunter, Founders of New Plymouth, 40–6.
11. History, 10.
12. Ibid. 11.
13. Ibid. 11.

CHAPTER IX.

1. For statements in this chapter see Bradford, History, 11–16.
2. Young, Chronicles, 465–6.

CHAPTER X.

1. Dexter, Congregationalism in Literature, 266 and note.
2. Ibid. 267, 277.
3. Ibid. 267–8.
4. Ibid. 263, etc.
5. Ibid. 278 and note.
6. Ibid. 310.
7. Ibid. 311–12, etc. Also True Story of John Smyth, the Se-Baptist [Lee & Shepard, 1881], 2, note 13.
8. So the university records state. But Professor Scheffer places these dates about ten years later, in 1586–93. De Brownisten, 78.
9. Dexter, True Story of John Smyth, 2, note 18.
10. Dexter, Congregationalism in Literature, 313–14.
11. Dialogue in Young, Chronicles, 455. Quoted by Dexter, Congregationalism in Literature, 317, with comments.
12. This has been disputed but seems established. See discussion by Dexter, True Story of John Smyth and Congregationalism in Literature, 319, note.
13. Dexter, Congregationalism in Literature, 318, note.
14. Bradford, History, 16–17.
15. Leyden Records, quoted by Dexter, Congregationalism in Literature, 383.
16. Dexter, Congregationalism in Literature, 331 and note.
17. Ibid. 270 and note. See also, for latest discoveries, Henry Ainsworth, the Puritan Commentator, by W. E. A. Axon and Ernest Axon, reprinted [1889] from Transactions of the Lancashire and Cheshire Antiquarian Society, 1888.
18. His commentary still is so valuable that the recent English revisers of the Old Testament made use of it. Dexter, Congregationalism in Literature, 342, note.

19. See Bibliography in Dexter's Congregationalism in Literature.

20. Dexter, Congregationalism in Literature, 325, etc.

CHAPTER XI.

1. Dexter, Congregationalism in Literature, 383.

2. One book known to have been printed by him is "a commentary on the Proverbs, by Cartwright, with a preface by Polyander, the Leyden Professor, 8vo, 1617." Hunter, Founders of New Plymouth, 137.

3. Various Leyden public records, marriage entries, etc., state their occupations.

4. See chapter vii. Also Dexter, Congregationalism in Literature, 387 and note.

5. The reasons establishing this conclusion are these: 1. There is no record of their worshiping anywhere else or of any grant to them by the authorities of a place of worship, which was sometimes made. 2. The Dutch government often confined the toleration of new and unusual sects to worship in private houses. 3. Robinson's burial in St. Peter's implies that they had no house of worship, or they would have buried him in it. 4. There is evidence that this house was too large and costly for them to have been likely to buy it except for use in worship. See Dexter, article "Pilgrims in Leyden," New England Magazine, September, 1889.

6. History, 17-18.

7. Ibid. 19-20.

8. Leyden Records.

9. Hypocrisie Vnmasked, etc., 95.

10. History, 21.

CHAPTER XII.

1. For statements in this chapter see Dexter, Congre-

gationalism in Literature, 98, 236, 314, etc., 325–6, 353, 392, etc., and 695.

2. Dexter speaks, Congregationalism in Literature, 328–9, of the "Elders" of the Leyden church but seems to be using the term loosely. Bradford, Dialogue in Young, Chronicles, 418, calls the same men "messengers" twice, which is exactly appropriate in the circumstances and corresponds to the modern term "delegates."

3. Works [Boston Tract Society, 1851], iii, 377.

CHAPTER XIII.

1. For statements in this chapter see Bradford, History, 23–44, 58–60.

2. See page 32.

3. Apparently the Pilgrims conceded so much as to consent to acknowledge some right of authority on the part of bishops duly appointed by the crown, but their language leaves it uncertain whether they referred to civil or ecclesiastical authority, and they insisted upon the right of a church to elect its own pastor, which claim neither king nor bishops were willing to admit. See the Seven Articles, quoted by J. A. Goodwin, Pilgrim Republic [Ticknor & Co, 1888], 41, and referred to by Sir Edwin Sandys, Bradford, History, 30.

4. Probably the latter is true. There is evidence that the English government tried to have him arrested for printing obnoxious religious books, that the Dutch felt obliged to assent, that one Thomas Brewer was apprehended by mistake, and that Brewster escaped to England safely and remained there and got off to America in the Mayflower undetected or at any rate unmolested. Goodwin, The Pilgrim Republic, 33.

CHAPTER XIV.

1. For statements in this chapter see Bradford, History, 57–78.
2. This is disputed, but Bradford, History, 70, says so plainly. Cushman afterwards was very useful to them in England.
3. Young, Chronicles, 98–9.
4. It is at least open to question if this date should not be November 20.
5. Dexter, Mourt's Relation, 2, note.

CHAPTER XV.

1. Dexter, Mourt's Relation, 7, note; 43, note.
2. Ibid. 44, note. Bradford, History, 330, 442, note.
3. Leyden Records. But Dexter, Mourt's Relation, 44, note, says May 26.
4. Dexter, Mourt's Relation, 13, note.
5. Ibid. 96, note. See also many allusions to him in Bradford's History.
6. Bradford, History, 264, note; 306, note. Dexter, Congregationalism in Literature, 415.
7. Bradford, History, 449.
8. Ibid. 89.
9. Bradford, Mourt's Relation, 5, 6.
10. Ibid. 6, 7, and note.

CHAPTER XVI.

1. Mourt's Relation, 3.
2. Bradford, History, 78.
3. Mourt's Relation, 13, etc.
4. Ibid, 27, etc.

5. Mourt's Relation, 43, note, says "one of Francis Billington's sonnes," which probably is an error. Bradford's list of the Mayflower Pilgrims (see preceding chapter) confirms this as an error by mentioning John, not Francis. So does Young's list, quoted from Prince, Annals of New England, 173, in Chronicles, 121–2. See also Chronicles, 214, note.

6. Mourt's Relation, 43, etc.
7. Ibid. 64.
8. Ibid. 84–5.

CHAPTER XVII.

1. For statements in this chapter see Mourt's Relation, 68–81, 91, etc. Also Bradford, History, 90–1.

2. Death reduced their numbers so rapidly that they did not need after all to build so many dwellings. Winslow says: "We have built seven dwelling houses and four for the use of the plantation" Young, Chronicles, 173, note. He seems to have meant that only seven dwellings for families were built, and it is quite likely that more than one house for general uses was needed.

3. Its exceptional severity has been disputed on the ground that the harbor is not recorded as having frozen over. But in any case it was much more inclement than any winter in their experience.

4. Young, Chronicles, 198–9, and notes. Palfrey, History of New England [Hurd & Houghton, 1866], i, 65. The statement rests only upon a tradition, but the tradition seems trustworthy. Abiel Holmes, Annals [W. Hilliard, 1805], 161, quoted by Young, Chronicles, 199, says that he personally had the fact from Ephraim Spooner, who had been told it by Thomas Faunce, who had been well acquainted with several of the Mayflower

company. There is the same authority, and only this, for the tradition that the Pilgrims first landed on Plymouth Rock.

5. Brewster and Standish were two of these. Young, Chronicles, 198.

CHAPTER XVIII.

1. For statements in this chapter see Bradford, History, 98–105, also Mourt's Relation, 98–130. The latter describes the three expeditions at some length.

2. A minister, a Mr. Crabe, had agreed to join them, apparently at Southampton, but did not. He was "much opposed," but whether by them or by his friends is not stated. Young, Chronicles, 85.

3. In March of this year one of this family, apparently its head, had been tried before the whole company for contempt of Captain Standish's orders and condemned "to have his neck and heels tied together."

4. On the general subject of the treatment of the Indians by the Pilgrims, see Young, Chronicles, 259 and note; also article "Did the Pilgrims Wrong the Indians?" Congregational Quarterly, i, 129–35; and C. F. Adams, Three Episodes of Massachusetts History [Houghton. Mifflin & Co., 1892], i, 100, etc.

CHAPTER XIX.

1. For statements in this chapter see Bradford, History, 105–12.

2. Young, Chronicles, 201.

3. Ibid. 280, note.

4. "Flankers" are projections built out so as to command the ground along the outside of a fence or wall and thus prevent an enemy from finding shelter there.

CHAPTER XX.

1. Bradford, History, 114.
2. Ibid. 118 and note; 123-4.
3. Ibid. 127.
4. Ibid. 138.
5. Ibid. 141.
6. Ibid. 142 and note.
7. Ibid. 116. This is a general statement. Bradford did not begin his history until about 1630. History, 6.
8. Ibid. 114.
9. Ibid. 125.
10. Ibid. 126.
11. Ibid. 137.
12. Ibid. 44.
13. Ibid. 134.
14. Ibid. 135.

CHAPTER XXI.

1. Bradford, History, 141, note.
2. Ibid. 113.
3. Ibid. 128.
4. Ibid. 131.
5. Ibid. 132. Adams gives details. Three Episodes, i, chapter vi.
6. Bradford, History, 126.
7. Ibid. 126, note.
8. Ibid. 413.
9. Although only an elder he probably wore the gown and bands while conducting worship, as they are included in the inventory of his possessions at his death. Goodwin, Pilgrim Republic, 34, note.
10. Bradford, History, 142.
11. Ibid. 143. Bradford's language is not quite clear. But his use of the word "company" seems to imply that they were to some extent organized, especially in view of

the fact that individual already had been substituted for common farming. If these new-comers merely had wished to labor each for his own account, the fact hardly would have been noted, because it would have involved no exception to what had become the custom.

12. Ibid. 146.
13. Ibid. 124–5.
14. Ibid. 128, etc.
15. Ibid. 133–4.
16. Ibid. 148–54.
17. Ibid. 154 and note. Adams, Three Episodes, i, 142–61.
18. Adams, Three Episodes, i, 142, 160–1, 322–8.
19. Bradford, History, 154.

CHAPTER XXII.

1. Bradford, History, 28, note. Adams, Three Episodes, 117.
2. Bradford, History, 41 and note.
3. Ibid. 43, 45 and note.
4. Ibid. 44, note.
5. Ibid. 107, note.
6. Ibid. 138–9.
7. Ibid. 107 and note.
8. Ibid. 117.
9. Ibid. 119–20.
10. Ibid. 157–8.
11. Ibid. 168 and note.
12. Ibid. 171–96.
13. Ibid. 196.
14. Ibid. 211–14.
15. Ibid. 250 and note.
16. Ibid. 289–90.
17. Ibid. 315.

Notes. 353

CHAPTER XXIII.

1. Bradford, History, 151 and note.
2. Ibid. 156.
3. W. T. Davis, Ancient Landmarks of Plymouth [A. Williams & Co., 1883], 76, 88.
4. Pilgrim Republic, 251.
5. Bradford, History, 157.
6. Ibid. 163, 165.
7. Ibid. 205-6.
8. Ibid. 215-17.
9. Ibid. 217. The frame of this ship is in the museum at Plymouth.
10. Ibid. 221.
11. Ibid. 222-5.
12. Ibid. 235-46. Adams, Three Episodes, i, chapters x-xv and xix.
13. Bradford, History, 169, note.
14. Ibid. 238, note. Adams, Three Episodes, i, 209.
15. Bradford, History, 264.
16. Ibid. 265-6 and note.
17. Ibid. 243.
18. Ibid. 263. Adams, Three Episodes, i, 230. Smith had come over from England to Salem with Higginson.
19. Bradford, History, 245-9. John Robinson's widow was not in either of these companies. Dr. Charles Deane, editor of the 1856 edition of Bradford's History, accepted the tradition that she was in one of them as "respectable" and thought that she came "with her son Isaac, and perhaps with another son." On the other hand Dr. Dexter said, in a note found among his papers after his death, "that no trace of her presence here was ever shown; that it is stated by a Dutch writer of the highest respectability [and] having means of knowledge that she never came; and that she is on record as still living in the Peterskerkhoff in Leyden in the spring of

1640, ten years after the date of her alleged arrival here." The Leyden record of course settles the point.

CHAPTER XXIV.

1. Bradford, History, 163–7.
2. Collections of the Massachusetts Historical Society, 1794, vol. iii.
3. There were only thirty-two in 1624. Davis, Ancient Landmarks, 55.
4. A storm "caused much daubing of our houses to fall down." Young, Chronicles, 179 and note.
5. Carpets had been imported into England for three quarters of a century or more, but hardly can have become common unless among the rich and luxurious.
6. Glass had been used in windows for some time, but, if they had provided any, it is probable that they would have sold it when they were paying their debts at Southampton before starting, rather than provisions, which we know that they sold. Moreover, Winslow wrote home, probably to George Morton, telling him to "bring paper and linseed oil for your windows with cotton yarn for your lamps." Young, Chronicles, 237–8.
7. See note 6.
8. Published in 1560, but not in England until 1575. "It very soon became the Bible of the household." Blackford Condit, History of English Bible [A. S. Barnes & Co., 1882], 241–51.
9. Dexter, Elder Brewster's Library, etc. [Proceedings of the Massachusetts Historical Society, 1889].
10. Even Elder Brewster owned at his death a violet coat and a green waistcoat. Goodwin, Pilgrim Republic, 34, note.
11. They did not use it for interments for some years. Burials probably were either on Cole's Hill, near the

rock, or upon their private grounds. Fort Hill was abandoned for defensive uses in 1679, and the oldest gravestone now standing, Edward Gray's, is dated 1681. Davis, Ancient Landmarks, 130–1.

12. The first cattle were brought over by Winslow in 1624. Bradford, History, 158.

13. Davis, Ancient Landmarks, 55.

14. Ibid. 107–8.

15. "After prayer" they had breakfast, etc., on their third exploring expedition from the ship. Young, Chronicles, 156.

16. They called the day the "Sabbath," or the "Lord's Day," or "First Day," objecting to "Sunday" as a title of heathen origin. Dexter, Congregationalism in Literature, 459.

17. William Palmer's will — he died in 1637 — bequeathed "somewhat towards ye meeting-house at Plymouth," as if one were being or about to be built. Plymouth Records.

18. A meeting somewhat of this character is recorded in Dedham as early as 1637, but nothing of the sort became generally customary until long afterwards. But the weekly lecture, "essentially a repetition of one Sabbath service," became usual in the Bay Colony almost as soon as the colony was established, and probably the Plymouth men had some meeting of this sort, at any rate after the first few years. In Boston it was held on Thursday and in the daytime. Dexter, Congregationalism in Literature, 456–7 and notes.

19. Ibid. 333.

20. i, 109.

CHAPTER XXV.

1. See chapter xxi, note 14.
2. Adams, Three Episodes, i, 183.

3. See chapter xxi, note 16.
4. Adams, Three Episodes, i, 161, 192.
5. Ibid. i, 161.
6. See chapter xxiii, note 12.
7. See chapter xxi, note 18.
8. See chapter xxiii, note 14.
9. Adams, Three Episodes, i, 218.
10. Ibid. i, 228.
11. Ibid. i, 233.
12. Cotton Mather, Magnalia, iii, 74.
13. T. Hutchinson, History of Massachusetts, i, 431.
14. Dexter, Congregationalism in Literature, 415-17. Professor Williston Walker, PH.D., The Influence of the Mathers in New England Religious Development [Proceedings of American Society of Church History, 1892], 63.
15. Massachusetts Colonial Records, i, 390. Quoted by Dexter, Congregationalism in Literature, 414.
16. Adams, Three Episodes, i, 230.
17. Massachusetts Colonial Records, i, 87. Quoted by Dexter, Congregationalism in Literature, 420.
18. Dexter, Congregationalism in Literature, 420. Adams, Three Episodes, ii, 815.
19. Adams, Three Episodes, i, 213-17.
20. Ibid. i, 382.
21. In 1633, John Doane, who had been made a deacon, was on this account voluntarily dropped from the Governor's council. Goodwin, Pilgrim Republic, 376, note.
22. Young, Chronicles, 126.
23. Bradford, History, 177.
24. Adams, Three Episodes, i, 364. Palfrey, History of New England, i, 106-7.
25. Bradford, History, 310. This passage is too long to be quoted here, but is very significant.

26. Douglas Campbell, The Puritan in England, Holland, and America [Harpers, 1892], ii, 142. Lauer, Church and State in New England [Johns Hopkins University Studies in Historical and Political Science, Tenth Series, ii–iii], 54–55.

27. Adams, Three Episodes, i, 245–6.

28. Ibid. 259–61.

29. Dexter, Congregationalism in Literature, 418. Palfrey, History of New England, i, 103. Lauer, Church and State in New England, 52.

CHAPTER XXVI.

1. Bradford, History, 264–6.

2. Page 1, note *a*.

3. Goodwin thinks that the only worship held in the several little colonies at the Bay up to this time had been in the Episcopal form. Pilgrim Republic, 318, 325–6.

4. Bradford, History, 266, note.

5. Page 57.

6. Page 58.

7. Dexter, Congregationalism in Literature, 484–5.

8. Ibid. 471, etc.

9. Ibid. 488, etc.

10. Ibid. 494, etc.

11. It should be noted here that it also is claimed by Professor Williston Walker, PH.D., — Creeds and Platforms of Congregationalism [Scribners, 1893], 492–4, — that the difference in the characters of the Governors and General Courts of Connecticut and Massachusetts at this time had much to do with the developments of Congregationalism in the two colonies. In the former colony civil interference in ecclesiastical affairs was customary and not specially unpopular.' But in Massachusetts this no longer was tolerated as it had been.

CHAPTER XXVII.

1. In 1679 twelve of the Mayflower Pilgrims themselves survived. History of Massachusetts, ii, 456. Quoted by Young, Chronicles, 3, note. The last survivor died in 1699. Goodwin, Pilgrim Republic, 476.

2. In 1643 it had formed — with the three other colonies of Massachusetts Bay, Connecticut, and New Haven — a league called The United Colonies of New England.

3. Quoted by T. W. Higginson, article "An English Nation," Harper's Magazine, April, 1883.

INDEX.

Achurch-cum-Thorpe, 44.
Adams, C. F., 350, 352, 353, 354, 356, 357.
Agawam. See Ipswich.
Ainsworth, Henry, 119, 121, 124, 127, 128, 144, 145.
Alden, John, 181, 184, 188.
Allerton, Isaac, 135, 182, 188, 212, 268, 269, 278, 280, 305.
Allerton, John, 188.
Anne, The, 184, 236, 250, 264.
Ashton, 343.
Austerfield, 69, 79.
Axon, W. E. A. and Ernest, 345.

Bacon, 339.
Barker, Elizabeth, 178.
Barrowe, Henry, 53, 55-58, 120, 122, 143.
Bassett, William, 132.
Basset Lawe, 98.
Bawtry, 69, 99.
Benet College, 37, 85.
Bibles, Wycliff's, 13; Tyndale's, 15; the Pilgrims', 294.
Billington, John, 188, 195, 349; Francis, 195, 349; John, 218.
Blackstone, William, 255, 302.
Blomefield, 338.
Bocking, 338.
Boston, in England, 108; in America, 302, 303; Proposals of Ministers of, 321.
Bowman, Christopher, 121.
Bradford, Thomas and Richard, 80; William, Sr., 79; William, Governor, 55, 70, 73, 79-82, 110, 112, 132, 135, 188, 192, 197, 204, 212, 216, 263, 268, 271, 273, 274, 280, 283, 286, 310, 318; Mrs. Dorothy, 81, 197.
Brewer, Thomas, 136, 348.

Brewster, William, Sr., 66, 73; Fear, 182; Jonathan, 78; Love, 78; Mary, 78; Prudence, 73; William, Elder, 66, 72-79, 97, 102, 110, 117, 132, 145, 158, 164, 188, 250, 273, 274, 283, 286, 293, 318, 348, 355; Wrestling, 78.
Bridewell Prison, 339.
Brill, 74.
Britteridge, Richard, 188.
Brydges, Sir Egerton, 99.
Bryne, James, 66.
Brook, 341.
Brown Alley, 129.
Brown, Dr. John, 338, 339; Peter, 188, 205.
Browne, Robert, 31, 36-49, 86, 142, 340.
Brownists, 32, 33, 153.
Browns, of Salem, 312.
Buckram, William, 97.
Burghley, Lord Treasurer, 40, 42.
Burial Hill, 248, 288.
Butten, William, 172.
Butter, Samuel, 132.
Butterfield, Stephen, 135.

Campbell, Douglas, 357.
Cape Cod, 173, 189, 200, 276.
Carpenter, Agnes, 184; Alice, 81, 98; Juliana, 100.
Cartwright, Thomas, 51, 143, 346.
Carver, John, Governor, 81, 157, 163, 164, 175-177, 188, 202, 204, 212; Catherine, 176.
Catherine, Queen, 13.
Chandler, Edmund, 135.
Charity, The, 235.
Charlestown, 220, 281, 301, 302, 303.
Chelsea, 301.

Cherbury, Lord Herbert of, 337.
Chilton, James, 188.
Chorley, 180.
Christ's College, 119, 122.
Clark, Richard, 188.
Clarke, 196.
Clark's Island, 196, 200.
Clifton, Richard, 80, 84, 87, 102, 295.
Clink Prison, 56.
Cole's Hill, 210, 355.
Colet, Henry, 135.
Collins, Henry, 132.
Colonial Records, Massachusetts, 356, 357.
Condit, Blackford, 355.
Congregationalism, Beginnings of, 30; First Church, 40; Early growth of, 142-150; Later growth of, 315-325.
Cook, Francis, 188, 206.
Copping, John, 41, 54, 340.
Corbitant, 219, 220.
Corpus Christi. See Benet.
Council, International Congregational, 69; National Congregational, 96; of New England, 268.
Crabe, 350.
Crackstone, John, 188.
Cromwell, 179.
Cushman, Robert, 78, 132, 157, 163, 164, 165, 168, 176, 223, 226, 227, 260, 265, 293, 348.
Cuthbertson, Cuthbert, 132.

Dartmouth, 167.
Davis, Hon. W. T., 353, 354, 355.
Davison, William, 73, 74, 75.
Day, Dr. G. E , 95.
Deane, Charles, 342, 354.
Dedham, 356.
Delfshaven, 161.
Dennis, William, 55.
De Rasieres, Isaac, 249, 250, 283.
D'Ewes, Sir S., 339.
Dexter, Dr. H. M., 67, 69, 95, 340-347, 354-356.
Discovery, The, 235.
Doane, John, 357.
Doncaster, 62.
Dorchester, 302.
Doten, Edward, 188, 229.
Dover, 302.
Droitwich, 177.

Dry Drayton, 38.
Duel, First, 229.
Duxbury, 181; Hall, 180.

East Boston, 301.
Eastham, 173.
Eaton, Francis, 188.
Edward VI, King, 15, 16.
Elizabeth, Queen, 17, 21, 74.
Ellis, Christopher, 135.
Elsivier, Baron, 343.
Endicott, John, 184, 279, 302, 317.
English, Thomas, 188.
Episcopius, Prof., 90, 136.
Evans, B., 341.

Faunce, Thomas, 350.
Fisher, Bishop, 14.
Fiske, John, 337.
Fitcher, 278.
Fitz, Richard, 339.
Fleet Prison, 120.
Fletcher, Rev. Henry, 70, 79; Moses, 188.
Flushing, 74.
Fort Hill, 288, 355.
Fortune, The, 78, 223, 224, 227, 263.
Froude, J. A., 337, 338.
Fuller, Edward, 188; Samuel, 132, 172, 183, 184, 188, 279, 287, 297, 317.

Gainsborough, 33, 61, 76, 85, 86, 123.
Gardiner, Richard, 188.
George, The, 302.
Glascock, Alice, 184.
Gloucester, 302.
Gonville and Caius College, 127.
Goodman, John, 188, 205.
Goodwin, J. A., 272, 347, 348, 352, 355, 357, 358.
Gorges, Captain Robert, 253, 254, 301.
Gott, Charles, 279.
Gray, Edward, 355; John, 301.
Green, J. R., 337, 338, 339.
Greene, William, 264.
Greenham, Rev. Richard, 38.
Greenwood, John, 55-58; John, 136.
Grey, Abraham, 135.
Grimsby, 62, 110.
Grindal, Archbishop, 66.

Index.

Hale, Dr. E. E., 341.
Hanson, Alice, 79; John, 79.
Hardy, Mary, 92.
Harrison, Robert, 39.
Heath, Archbishop, 66.
Helwys, 126.
Henry V, King, 13.
Henry VIII, King, 13, 14, 65.
Higginson, Rev. Francis, 306, 354; T. W., 358.
Hobomok, 219, 247.
Holmes, Abiel, 350.
Hopkins, Oceanus, 173; Stephen, 173, 188, 217, 229, 230.
Houghton, Lord, 67.
Howland, John, 172, 188.
Hull, 110.
Humber, 111.
Hunt, Captain Thomas, 207.
Hunter, Rev. Joseph, 65, 80, 97, 98, 99, 342, 344, 346.
Hutchinson, Governor T., 328, 356; Mrs. Anne, 313.

Idle River, 71.
Ipswich, 195.
Islington, 26, 37.
Ivimey, J., 341.

Jackson, Richard, 97.
James I, King, 21, 65, 122, 158, 187.
Jennings, John, 132.
Jepson, Henry, 136; William, 88, 135.
Jessop, Edmund, 132; Francis, 98, 102, 135.
Johnson, Rev. Francis, 56, 119-128, 295; Mrs. Francis, 121, 125; George, 119-122.
Jones, 193, 194.

Keble, John, 135.
Kennebec, 269.
Knight, Walter, 301.
Knyveton, George, 121.

Laud, Archbishop, 178.
Lauer, 357.
Lee, Bridget, 184; Samuel, 132.
Leicester, Earl of, 74.
Leister, Edward, 188, 229.
Leland, 65.
Lever, Thomas, 339.
Leyden, 88, 126, 130, 139; Records, 80, 97, 100, 131, 346; University Registers, 85, 343.

Libraries, 286-7.
Little James, 236, 250, 265.
Liverpool, 62.
Lollards, 13.
London Company. See Merchant Adventurers.
Lyford, John, 266, 310, 311.

Manomet. See Sandwich.
Margaret, Queen, 65.
Margeson, Edmond, 188.
Mar-prelate, Martin, tracts, 53.
Marshall, William, 66.
Martin, Christopher, 164, 188.
Mary, Bloody Queen, 16; Queen of Scots, 74; and John, The, 302.
Massasoit, 207, 217, 219, 247, 248.
Massingberd, 337, 338.
Masterson, Richard, 132.
Mather, Rev. Cotton, 356; Rev. Richard, 319.
Maverick, Samuel, 301.
May, 32; Dorothy, 81.
Mayflower, 135, 160, 162, 167, 169, 193, 194, 196, 197, 202, 213.
Medford, 303.
Merchant Adventurers, 159, 164, 225-6, 234, 242, 258-269, 305.
Merry Mount, 181, 277.
Middleburg, 40.
Minter, Desire, 176.
Mishawum. See Charlestown.
Monhegan, 255.
More, Chancellor, 14; Richard, 78.
Morell, Rev. William, 254, 255.
Morton, George, 99-101, 102, 236, 354; Nathaniel, 342; Thomas, 277-279, 302, 312.
Mullins, Priscilla, 181, 185; William, 188.

Nantasket, 266, 267, 302.
Narragansetts, The, 230-31, 247.
Nauset, 218.
Neal, 32, 337, 338, 339; Elizabeth, 97.
New Netherlands, 277.
Noddle's Island. See East Boston.
Norfolk, Duke of, 37.
Northampton, 43, 45.

Northern Company, 257, 261.
Norris, Mary, 182.
Norwich, 39, 40.

Oldham, 266, 267, 309, 311.
Orleans, 173.

Palfrey, 350, 357.
Palmer, William, 355.
Pamet River, 192.
Pecksuot, 248.
Peirce, John, 235, 262.
Penn, Admiral, 179.
Penry, John, 53, 55, 58-9, 118.
Pesijn, Jan, 343.
Pickering, Edward, 132, 264.
Piscataqua, 255.
Plantation, The, 236.
Pluygers, Professor, 343.
Plymouth, in England, 167, 258;
 in America, 196, 197, 200, 249,
 252, 253, 254, 255, 263, 269,
 278, 280, 296.
Plymouth Colony, 304.
Plymouth Company, 258.
Poliander, 136, 346.
Popham, Judge, 340, 341.
Priest, Digory, 135, 188.
Prince, 349.
Provincetown, 173, 189.
Psalms, Ainsworth's, 294.

Quadequina, 207.

Rainea, 121.
Raleigh, Sir Walter, 32.
Ratcliff, Philip, 312.
Rathband, W., 316.
Reinolds, 166.
Rich, Lord Robert, 55.
Ridgdale, John, 188.
Robinson, Rev. John, 82, 84-
 96, 110, 117, 130, 136, 145,
 160, 166, 273, 274, 283, 339,
 343; Mrs. John, 354.
Rochester, Robert, 97.
Rochford, 55.
Rogers, Rev. Mr., 280.
Rogers, Thomas, 135, 188.
Rough, 26.
Roxbury, 303.
Ryton River, 64, 68, 71.

Salem, 279, 281, 302, 303, 307.
Samoset, 207.
Sandwich, 276.
Sandys, Archbishop, 66; Sir
 Edward, 347; Sir Samuel, 66.

Savage, Archbishop, 65.
Saybrook Synod, 322.
Scrooby, 61, etc., 72, 73, 74.
Shawmut. See Boston.
Simpson, 27.
Skeats 337, 339.
Slade, M., 121.
Smith, Rev. Ralph, 280, 296,
 307, 312, 354.
Smyth, Rev. John, 61, 87, 122-
 126, 128, 148, 149, 345.
Soule, George, 188.
Southampton, 162, 163, 166.
Southwark, 37, 44.
Southworth, Edward, 98, 132;
 Mrs. Alice, 81, 98.
Sparrow, The, 235.
Speedwell, The, 160, 166-168.
Spooner, Ephraim, 350.
Squanto, 207, 213, 217, 219, 220,
 247.
Squantum, 220.
Stamford, 42.
Standish, Captain Miles, 180-
 182, 188, 191, 195, 206, 220,
 248, 268, 273, 278, 287, 310,
 350; Barbara, 181; Rose, 180.
Stock Company, 275.
Strype, 337, 339.
Studley, Daniel, 121.
St. Helen's Church, 70, 79.
St. John's College, 127.
St. Olave's School, 44.
St. Pancras and St. Mary's
 Church, 140.
St. Peter's Church, 88, 93, 96,
 140.
St. Wilfred's Church, 62.
Sumner, George, 69.
Swansea, 218.
Swanton Morley, 127.

Tarratines, The, 220.
Taylor, A., 341.
Thacker, Elias, 41, 54, 340.
Thickins, Randall, 88.
Thoroton, 67.
Tilley, Edward, 188; John, 188.
Tilne, 98.
Tinker, Thomas, 135, 188.
Truro, 191.
Tulloch, 337, 338.
Turner, John, 135, 188.

Venable, General, 179.
Virginia Company, 158, 257,
 258, 260.

Index. 363

Walker, Dr. Williston, 339, 356, 358.
Warren, Richard, 188.
Warwick, Earl of, 268.
Watertown 267, 302.
Waymouth, Capt. George, 207.
Wellfleet, 195.
Wessagusset. See Weymouth.
West, Captain Francis, 236.
Weston, Thomas, 159, 164, 165, 226, 252-254, 259, 263, 264.
Weymouth, 248, 252, 253, 264, 301.
White, Frances, 98; Peregrine, 193; Roger, 274; Susannah, 178, 215; Thomas, 122; William, 188, 216.
Williams, Roger, 296, 311, 313; Thomas, 188.
Wilson, Rev. John, 297, 303; Roger, 132.
Wincob, John, 258.
Winnisimmet. See Chelsea.
Winslow, Edward, 132, 137, 177-180, 188, 208, 215, 217, 238, 264, 265, 343, 349, 355; Elizabeth, 216; Gilbert, 188.
Winthrop, Governor John, 296, 297, 302, 303.
Wise, Rev. John, 323.
Wituwamat, 248.
Wollaston, Captain, 277, 302; Mount, 277, 278, 302.
Wolsey, Cardinal, 68.
Wood, Henry, 88.
Worksop, 98.
Wycliff, 13.

York, 62.
York, Archbishopric of, 68.
Young, 341-343, 347-351, 354-358.

www.ingramcontent.com/pod-product-compliance
Lightning Source LLC
Chambersburg PA
CBHW071225230426
43668CB00011B/1309